LITTLE FARM FOR THE HOLIDAYS

CELEBRATING THE CHRISTMAS SEASON HOMESTEAD-STYLE, WITH AN IRISH CHRISTMAS NOVELETTE

LITTLE FARM IN THE FOOTHILLS
BOOK FIVE

SUSAN COLLEEN BROWNE

LITTLE FARM FOR THE HOLIDAYS

Celebrating the Christmas Season Homestead-Style

Susan Colleen Browne

Little Farm for the Holidays

Copyright © 2024 and 2025 by Susan Colleen Browne

All rights reserved. No part of this book may be used or reproduced in any form without written permission except as brief quotations or excerpts in critical articles and reviews.

Some names of persons appearing in this book have been changed to protect their privacy.

ebook ISBN: 978-1-952470-21-9

Print ISBN: 978-1-952470-23-3

The Christmas Visitor

Copyright © 2011 and 2022 by Susan Colleen Browne

This is a work of fiction. Names, characters, places, and incidents either are the product of the author's imagination or are used fictitiously, and resemblance to actual persons, living or dead, business establishments, events, or locales is entirely coincidental.

The Christmas Visitor ebook ISBN: 978-0-9816077-8-8

Published by Whitethorn Press

Cover Design by Whitethorn Press

Cover photographs © John F. Browne

www.susancolleenbrowne.com

www.susancolleenbrowne.substack.com

ALSO BY SUSAN COLLEEN BROWNE

Village of Ballydara Series

It Only Takes Once

Mother Love

The Hopeful Romantic

The Galway Girls

The Secret Well

The Christmas Visitor

The Little Irish Gift Shop

Becoming Emma

Becoming Emma: Special Edition with Two Ballydara Short Stories

The Fairy Cottage of Ballydara

Memoir and Gardening

Little Farm in the Foothills: A Boomer Couple's Search for the Slow Life

Little Farm Homegrown: A Memoir of Food-Growing, Midlife and Self-Reliance on a Small Homestead

Little Farm in the Garden: A Practical Mini-Guide to Raising Selected Fruits and Vegetables Homestead-Style

Little Farm in the Henhouse: A True-Life Tale of Hen-Keeping Homestead-Style

Middle Grade Fiction

Morgan Carey and The Curse of the Corpse Bride

Morgan Carey and The Mystery of the Christmas Fairies

The Secret Astoria Scavenger Hunt

To John, who brought Christmas back to me

COZY SEASON

"I'm thankful to live in a place where winter gets good and cold and you need to build a fire in a stove and wrap a blanket around you. Cold brings people closer together."

—Garrison Keillor

As Christmas draws nearer, and the winter's chill sets in, life seems to take on a whole new tenor.

If you live in the Northern hemisphere, in the dark days leading to the winter solstice it seems natural to live more attuned to the slower rhythms of the season. At our little homestead, choosing calming, comfy pastimes is how my husband John and I like to get into holiday mode: baking goodies, taking easy walks down our quiet rural lane, and of course, reading books.

If you're a big reader like me, I think choosing something

uplifting is both comforting *and* relaxing, and the reason I created this little book.

As for other cozy activities…when I discovered the Danish notion of *hygge*, I realized, "Goodness—I've been doing this for years!"

You've probably heard of *hygge*—it looks like it could be pronounced "higgee," "huggee" or with a little stretch of imagination, "hug me"…but I understand it's pronounced "hoo-ga." However you say it, *hygge* really speaks to me this time of year. From what I gather, this Danish practice is all about treating yourself to extra light, comforting food, and cheerful activities —embracing anything that gives you a sense of contentment.

In fact, starting in November, adopting "*hygge*-forward" activities is a great workaround for our Foothills' cold weather and frequent power outages.

You might consider this *hygge* lifestyle as socially acceptable —and even healthy—couch potato-ing: maybe curling up with a warm throw blanket, bathed in candlelight, with a mug of hot cocoa at the ready.

On a cold night, John and I think there's nothing better than preparing comfort foods like homemade soup or chocolate chip cookies. Then after dinner, lolling in front of a crackling fire in the woodstove, immersed in a good book really hits the spot! But really, you might consider *hygge* any simple, even homespun pursuit that dials up your happiness and wellbeing—especially at holiday time.

Over the years, even before we moved to the country, I've made a conscious effort to simplify the holidays for John and me. Instead of trying to do more shopping, cooking, baking, entertaining, and attending events than feels comfortable, we like to focus on light and warmth. Which coincidentally, is what *hygge* is all about.

Too, avoiding the stress of *too much*, we've leaned into a greater appreciation for holiday dishes that aren't elaborate, small, if meaningful gifts, and undemanding (and even a little humble) rituals.

Does that sound unrealistic? Maybe our lives here on our little farm seem a little too idealized to some people. Or out of the mainstream. John and I don't use cell phones, because there's no cell reception for miles around. Also: we don't want to! We don't have streaming services, because our satellite internet doesn't have enough bandwidth for Netflix or Apple TV.

John and I generally don't go to town more than once or twice a week—and often wish we never had to leave! We're also old-school enough to be friends with—and sometimes depend upon—our neighbors.

So we do keep things pretty simple generally—out of choice *and* necessity.

This simpler mindset has served us well, given our ever-shifting home and extended family landscape. Like John and me, I'm sure you've experienced the many ups and downs of elderly parents, grown children and grandkids, and job and financial worries. Then there's the vagaries of winter weather and power outages. All in all, those unexpected twists and turns have taught us that the best-laid plans often go awry.

So if I've learned anything about our holiday celebrations, it's to stay flexible…and not get too invested in any single ritual or activity.

If you have loved ones close by, maybe this slow season might give you a bit more time to cuddle your kids or your sweetie or your pets—an easy way to create a sense of wellbeing! Being the grandparent of little children, I've rediscovered that something as basic as holding a baby is akin to a spiritual experience.

I've also learned that simplicity not only makes life easier at holiday-time, but that it may be a pathway to something beyond the everyday.

That's why I've included my Irish novelette, ***The Christmas Visitor***, in this book. It's a tender, mystical story that takes place the night before Christmas Eve. You'll find ***The Christmas Visitor*** at the end of ***Little Farm for the Holidays***.

And finally…perhaps, not getting too "fussed" as Scottish people might say, you'll find opportunities to open your heart… to get a glimpse of the mystical elements of Christmas. Whatever your life may hold, it's my hope that these tales will add a bit of old-fashioned spirit and cheer to your Christmas season.

WARM WISHES,

Susan

THE MAGIC OF CHRISTMAS

Feeling a sense of awe, to me, is a gift of being human. It's that glimpse of something larger than ourselves, of having that sense of the miraculous—that somehow, through forces we will never understand, we are alive on an isolated chunk of rock spinning through the vastness of the Universe.

It's those moments when I see a shooting star, view our rare Aurora borealis, or find myself in the presence of something sublimely beautiful, like the slanting pink light on the Foothills at sunset. Or the sweetness in a baby's face.

Yet call it serendipity, or synchronicity, there are some things you might experience, or "miracles" you hear about, that make your spine tingle a little—because they can't be explained by rational thought or science. Or even common sense.

If this serendipity happens at Christmas, it feels like a gift, doesn't it?

Yet these magical or other-worldly experiences don't need to be confined to holiday traditions. As someone attuned to all things Irish, I've come across some spine-tingling Irish stories.

I had an interesting student in one of my creative writing

classes. Her mother's grandmother came from Ireland, with the surname of Quinn. This mother, an American, had recurring dreams all her life of an old castle ruin with crumbling steps. Later in life, she went to Ireland on a tour, and the bus stopped at a castle.

Exploring the grounds, this woman saw those same steps she'd seen in her dreams. The name of the castle? Castle Quinn.

An old friend of mine, an Irish-American author, took her first trip to Ireland some years ago. Before the aircraft landed, she gazed down at the green hills of the Emerald Isle below and was completely overcome by the conviction that she *belonged* there. The sensation was so powerful, she said, "I felt like I could have jumped right out of the plane."

In the compelling memoir *Midlife Irish*, Irish-American journalist Joe Gannon visited Ireland to look up his ancestors. During his first trip, Gannon says that wherever he went, he felt this overwhelming sense that heaven, or the life beyond this one, was as close as the next room. Some Irish people describe it as places where "the veil is thin."

Was the recurring dream of my student's mother, or my friend's sense of belonging, or the journalist's mystical sense simply the mind playing tricks Or it is possible they were some kind of message from beyond?

Science can't prove these kinds of other-worldly sensations and experiences are real…but can belief?

Even if these three anecdotes aren't Christmas stories, they remind me that if you keep an open mind and heart, Christmastime—and the entire holiday season (whatever holiday you may be celebrating)—is brimming with magic and mystery.

As we know, the legend of St. Nicholas—who represents the simpler, old-fashioned holidays you may secretly yearn for—isn't *all* fiction…

He was a real-life bishop in 4th century Turkey. After performing many extraordinarily kind and generous deeds, Church fathers named him the patron saint of children. Later, this historical figure emerged from the mists of time to became mythical—a benevolent spirit who left treasure and gifts in children's shoes or stockings.

Over the centuries, this mythical presence evolved to include Father Christmas and Santa Claus, as well as other magical beings of other countries and other cultures—all of whom represent the spirit of love and generosity.

And little children around the world believe in this magical spirit as strongly and as fervently as they believe in *anything*, long after they're old enough to know the difference between reality and make believe.

One Christmas Eve, when I was seven, I was watching *The Laurence Welk* show with my beloved grandma in our basement rec room. Suddenly, I heard some strange thumping upstairs. Within moments, my dad called down to us, "Santa was just here!" As I tore up the stairs, I believed…no, I *knew* it was Santa who'd made that noise and left those presents. There was simply no other explanation.

"Seeing isn't believing; believing is seeing." —Judy the Elf, from the movie *The Santa Clause*

So as long as you *believe*, a little bit, in being open to the awe and wonder of the season, everywhere you look you'll find a little bit of St. Nick's magic.

"FALLIDAYS" AND FAITH

*D*oesn't it seem like the holiday windup is starting earlier and earlier?

These days, the Christmas season swings into gear in October. Candy canes and chocolate Santas are on the store shelves by Halloween, and the Hallmark Channel kicks off their holiday movie lineup the third week of October. But the little farm town where John and I go to the bank and library are real early birds: they've got their holiday street decor up by mid-month!

I've noticed a lot of holiday yard lights in early November. Yet the traditional Christmas season, which has generally begun right after Thanksgiving dinner, still feels a bit early to me. If you put up your Christmas tree that weekend, an artificial one will be dusty and bedecked with spider webs by Christmas Eve. A real fir will be pale and dried out by the big day too.

As for your holiday spirit, if you ramp it up too soon, all those warm fuzzies, like a Christmas tree, could be worn out before you start opening presents!

But then, I'm a longtime empty nester. If I still had young children in my house, I know enough about popular culture that the Elf on the Shelf, that post-Thanksgiving must-do ritual, would *not* be optional. Since I don't, I can take a little breather between my Thanksgiving and Christmas dinners.

On the other hand, there is such a thing as waiting too long—like the people who don't do any shopping or other holiday preparations until a couple of days before Christmas.

When I was a child, with two busy working parents, Christmas always seemed very last-minute. Ours was always the last family in the neighborhood to put up a tree. I would actually get a little anxious, waiting for my dad to string outdoor lights on the shrubbery, and for anything else Christmasy to happen for our family. By the time I was a teen, my parents actually did postpone buying gifts until Christmas Eve.

If Thanksgiving feels a bit too early to start my serious holiday prep, and just before Christmas is too late, December 6th seems *just right*. St. Nicholas Day. And while John and I haven't "believed" in Santa since we were little, the legend of this important saint inspires our holidays.

You may be wondering, why *St. Nicholas*? I'll explain with a little story…

At a recent author event, a visitor came to my table, an attractive, bubbly mom with a beautiful smile. We chatted for a bit, then she gestured at all the titles on my table, and asked me how I came to write different kinds of books—my Little Farm gardening and homesteading books, my Irish novels, and my middle-grade fantasy-adventure stories.

"Oh, that's a good question," I said. "I just write as the spirit moves."

Her eyes seemed to brighten. She asked, "Are you a Christian?" She wore a pretty wooden cross around her neck.

For a moment, I wasn't sure how to answer. But I could just be honest. "I was raised Presbyterian and Catholic," I told her. "I don't go to church these days, but…" Without planning it, I put my hand on my heart. "It's always with me."

She looked uncertain. "I hope it's okay I asked—it's just that when you said 'spirit,' I wondered…"

"Of course it's okay," I told her. I was actually quite honored she'd posed the question. "I saw your lovely necklace."

Her son made it for her, she said, and we parted ways, smiling. Other people came to my table, so I didn't get a chance to reflect on what I'd shared. Now, this being a book about Christmas, it seems right to do it here.

In my earlier childhood, my dad took us to an imposing old stone Presbyterian church for Sunday School. He never spoke to us about religion or faith, but he was so faithful about never letting us miss a Sunday, my siblings and I used to win Sunday School attendance awards.

Later, while I was still in elementary school, through a strange turn of events my two sisters and I had our first Holy Communion. As I grew up, my Catholic church attendance dwindled—as did my sisters'—right along with my parents' commitment to taking their kids to church. Still, I'm part of the generation that experienced school Christmas parties and sang carols for the school Christmas program.

Many years (decades!) later, and carrying much of that faith in my heart, I gravitate toward rituals and stories that reflect the traditional Christmases of my childhood. The old-fashioned carols, the Nativity and eternal Christmas story in the Scriptures, and the saints' feast days. Christmas cards featuring a small, steepled church in the middle of the woods.

On Christmas Eve, if the night sky is clear, I've been known to search for a bright star in the east.

Yet the many other fall and winter holidays of other faiths and cultures, each with their own special rituals and food and symbols, sing to me too. When all's said and done, these festivities, that celebrate light, family, community and the spirit of generosity, seem like the finest gifts we could ever wish for.

SAINT NICHOLAS DAY

The Feast Day of St. Nicholas, December 6th, is, as I said, a special day for John and me. Even though I don't *completely* wait until the sixth to swing into holiday mode.

December 1st is the day I begin to *ease* into the holidays (as befits our slower lifestyle!). My first tradition is to pull out my three Advent calendars. All three depict a Nativity scene—two are set a medieval cathedral, and one shows a rather unlikely snowy landscape in what must be the Bethlehem of antiquity.

Made in Germany, the calendars are adorned with glitter, and since I bought them around 1983, I suppose they could be considered vintage. I have loved these calendars through the years, though they've faded over time, and lose more and more glitter each season.

Still, as I open the first little paper window, my anticipation rises, like it does every year. Inside, there's a tiny human figure or angel, along with a snippet of Scripture from the Christmas story. I always like to pause a moment, and meditate on the lovely verse I just read.

Once the Advent calendars are up, I'll give it a couple of days before starting the next stage: clearing the books and photos off the shelves and tabletops to make room for our holiday tchotchkes, candles and knickknacks, and actually *dust* every surface. (That's worth celebrating in itself!) The bare spaces seem a little bereft …but maybe they too, are anticipating being bedecked in the very near future.

But the 6th is our *official* kickoff for the holiday season. That's when John and I begin making merry…that is, in our low-key homesteady-style.

That day, the Feast Day of St. Nicholas, I pull my favorite holiday book out of my closet—*Believe: A Christmas Treasury* by Mary Engelbreit is an illustrated collection of some of the loveliest songs, scripture, stories and traditions from around the world. The book is filled with all kinds of ways to create fun and meaningful celebrations. I'll keep it on the coffee table, so I can re-read a few selections every night throughout the season, until Epiphany.

Once the workday is over, I haul our plastic bin of Christmas knickknacks out of the deep recesses of our main storage closet. Before setting them out, I'll put on the only Christmas music I ever play: gentle, old-Englishy choral music like "In the Bleak Midwinter" or "Wexford Carol."

To me, the old-fashioned carols bring a certain softness and spiritual mood to the season. But if you want a combination of traditional and lively, a rousing tune like "Wassail Song" will surely inspire a joyful exuberance in any holiday activity! The lyrics are all about toasting your farm animals and the New Year, and sharing what's really important: a good crop of corn, a piece of meat, and your Christmas pie. And of course, your bowl of wassail.

The song reminds me that in days gone by, people centered their holiday celebrations around feasting on special food and drink. Not presents.

Once the old carols gently waft through the house, it's finally time to decorate. Through the years, John has been the one to gift our family with holiday décor—my favorite store-bought ones are two ceramic angels, and a large snow globe depicting the Nativity, with a music box inside that plays "O Come All Ye Faithful."

Arranging the knickknacks and Nativity figurines, and setting strings of colored lights on the windowsills gives me that same anticipatory glow I get from opening that first Advent window. Finally, John and I hang up the two beautiful Christmas tapestries he chose a few years back. Newly decorated, our place feels infused with holiday cheer.

Our house is nothing like the homes of collector-type folks you see in magazines, who cover every inch of what's always a really big house with holiday figurines, lights, candles, greenery, swags, bows, wreaths…and on and on. And *on*.

True, these lavish, picture-perfect decorations look festive. Yet it seems to me that with your house stuffed to the rafters, any items of sentimental value, like the family treasures passed down through the generations, or the tree ornaments your child made for you when they were little, gets lost in the shuffle.

With the tapestries up, and the decorating finished (until we put up a tree around the 16th), I'll gaze for a long moment at my decades-old, child-made knickknacks. To me, they're priceless: the small red felt disc with a bit of shiny green garland glued to it, surrounding a wee photo of one of my daughters at five years old. My younger daughter's finest creation is a clear globe with dried pink flowers artistically glued on it, with a slightly crooked "MOM" spelled out in silver glitter. Both are a bit battered from time. But they still get a place of honor, where I can see them best.

After decorating, to make the day even more special, I'll mix up our first batch of holiday cookies, and John and I will bake them together.

For me, part of the "magic" in those treasured decorations and cookie-making is the gift of nostalgia—all the feelings inspired by the special items you haven't seen since last January, the special treats you haven't had all year, or the tiny angels behind the windows of a faded Advent calendar.

And I think that "believing," according to Judy the Elf, is sensing that angels *do* exist. St. Nicholas surely must be one. And perhaps so are people whose spirits are imbued with goodness—the especially kind and generous people we know or have known. If believing is seeing, maybe those special people have come into our lives for a *reason*.

If I had a real-life angel in my life, it was my Laurence Welk-watching grandma. But sometimes, especially at Christmastime, you're lucky enough to witness the blessings of other angels.

ANGELS AMONG US

I was in our little farm town's post office one December afternoon, to mail our Christmas package to John's daughter. For such a small community, it's a good-sized P.O., so you rarely have to wait. But on this day, there was only one counter open, with at least a dozen folks in line with parcels to ship.

A little family stepped up to the counter, a thirty-something mom, a pretty young teen, and a little girl, all with the same shade of blond hair. The mother spoke English with a heavy accent—I guessed they were Ukrainian, since there's a sizeable immigrant community of Ukrainian folks in the Foothills.

The mom and the teen set a couple of large, bedraggled boxes on the counter to send out. The post office clerk added up the postage, then affixed the stickers to the boxes. "Ready to go," he said. "That'll be $27.53."

The mother seemed to hesitate, then swiped her debit card.

The card reader emitted a sharp tone: a "no" in machine-speak. The postal worker, very politely, said, "Here, swipe it again." Same result: the machine wouldn't accept the card. Then *he* swiped it—to no avail.

The little girl, sensing her mother's distress, I guessed, huddled against her. Finally, the clerk attempted the transaction by manually entering her card number into his system. Still, the card was a no-go.

"I'm sorry," he said, sounding honestly sympathetic. "I'm going to have to tear the stickers off, unless you can come back in a few minutes with cash or check." Despite all the people lined up, the lobby was silent. You couldn't help but hear the mother's soft, embarrassed murmurs—and feel the discomfort among the other customers.

Then all of a sudden, a forty-something woman stepped up to the counter. "I've got it."

The mother said, "Oh, no—I can't—"

"Random act of kindness," the woman said briskly. "I've got it."

She literally would not let the mother to say no. The tension in the little family eased.

You could see the clerk visibly relax too as he took the other woman's card; in fact, I could feel everyone in the lobby relax. I did as well, tears brimming in my eyes.

The guy next to me in line said, "There's been a lot of that lately—random acts of kindness. It's been on the news." In that moment, I felt the holiday spirit pervade the entire room. I'm sure this generous woman had *made* Christmas for that little family. And this lovely person, whom I'd never seen before and would likely never see again, totally made *my* Christmas too.

A half hour later, still feeling a little teary from the kindness I'd witnessed, I was driving into the city, listening to the radio. Garrison Keillor and his "Writer's Almanac" came on the air. After reciting his usual notable birthdays, and a lovely poem, Keillor shared a final thought—a quote from author Arthur C. Clarke:

"Just think of how peaceful the world would be if we all treated each other as if we were members of the same family."

That day in the post office, the dozen or so people in the small lobby had indeed become a family. And in those few moments, you could feel the humble Christmas verse come alive—there truly was "peace on earth and good will toward men."

O CHRISTMAS TREE

What do you love best about the Christmas season?

If you love the holidays like I do, it's impossible to choose! But if I had to come up with something… What makes Christmas so special to me is the lights and sparkle, the celebratory pause before winter's long, cold slog, and most of all, the spiritual aspects of the most profound Christmas stories.

Some of the oldest holiday traditions, like bringing evergreens into your house, are the ones I hold most dear. I always thought this indoor greenery originated several centuries ago, in Germany and the Scandinavian countries.

Yet I recently learned the evergreen custom can be traced much further back—to ancient Rome, and even Egypt. In those long-ago times, evergreens symbolized *life*: vibrantly green throughout the year, this foliage gave hope that spring—and its warmth and sunlight for food crops—would return.

And while John and I focus on simple holiday traditions, I've always had one requirement, no ifs, ands or buts:

Not only greenery in the house, but a Christmas tree. A *real* one.

For the first decade of our married life, every December, around mid-month, we purchased a tree. And not just any tree: a seven-foot fir. To me, Christmas wasn't Christmas unless I had an oversized, fully decorated *real* tree in my living room, exuding that lovely scent of fresh fir.

We would set it up the week before Christmas—and there it would stay until Epiphany, January 6. At least! Happily, John was totally on board about keeping our tree up for this extended time, until the needle-drop became extreme.

Embracing the country vibe even before we moved out of the city, we eventually let go of grocery store "They-cut" firs and began a new tradition: venturing out to a rural Christmas tree farm for a "U-cut."

Douglas fir was the affordable option, but once every few years John and I would *really* go all out, and spend the big bucks for a noble or grand fir. Even in the Pacific Northwest, where firs are plentiful, a noble or grand would fetch top dollar.

As the years rolled on, seven-footers seemed a bit unwieldy. I managed to let go of my must-have *huge* tree, and dialed it down… To a six-foot fir. But a few years ago, my usual holiday plans—including my precious tree tradition— were turned upside down.

John and I were needed for an out-of-town family emergency.

Without a spare second to bake a few cookies or buy some gifts—and of course Christmas cards were completely off the table—I was forced to make do. Just before we had to leave home, I managed to create a Christmas tree…of sorts.

I'd had my eye on a stand of baby cedar trees on our property, which were growing too close together to thrive. That rainy December day, I cut down three of the saplings. Once home, I lashed them together, and stuck their spindly little trunks in a sturdy vase filled with water.

Even with the foliage of three baby trees, the little cedars were decidedly reminiscent of a "Charlie Brown" Christmas tree, sparse and a bit sad. Kind of a "semi-tree." Cedars being rather soft and flexible, the tree didn't really support our decorations properly.

I felt a bit bereft, having to severely pare down the lights and tchotchkes. I missed seeing our angel ornament collection, the crystal icicles, all my shiny, glittery ornaments. Yet in a way, dialing down my tree tradition, and letting go of all that shiny stuff turned out to have an unexpected result.

I gained a new appreciation for my more homely but cherished items—the ones with personal meaning. Like the crafty ones my daughters had made when they were little, memories imbued in the glue and glitter. And the wee Snoopy decoration my sister gave me, which was suddenly so perfect for this Charlie Brown tree.

Simplifying my tree tradition had actually been positive. And that holiday season, while we were away, I found myself longing for the sight of my little improvised tree.

Once this emergency had passed, Christmas Day had come and gone. By the time we arrived home after a fraught drive on the icy interstate, my three little trees were deader than Jacob Marley of *A Christmas Carol*.

It was clear I couldn't keep this fire hazard in my living room until Epiphany. But we had bigger problems. Our water system had completely frozen while we were away, and would remain so for five long days.

But I just *knew* I could redeem myself for next Christmas. Get a proper Christmas tree.

The following Christmas, however, my plans for our usual tree once again hit a snag. Just before the holidays, the dear little out-of-town family we had helped last year came down with severe flu—every single person!—and needed a full-time helper.

This flu was a week-long illness, but thankfully, everyone finally recovered—the one bright spot of the season. John and I returned home to an unwelcome surprise—the second year in a row. This time, a series of unfortunate events cascaded into our lives like mountain waterfall after a rainstorm.

Mice had invaded our kitchen pantry, we had a leak in the shop that had created an indoor skating rink, and the next day, while I was organizing and sanitizing our pantry shelves, a cold front/blizzard hit the Foothills, like none we'd ever seen before.

With three feet of snow on the ground, and temperatures in the single-digits, John and I would not be going anywhere. As it was, the snow was too deep to hike into the woods to locate even a marginal tree. The best I could do tree-wise was arrange a string of lights around our leggy indoor hibiscus, park a few ornaments on it, and as John would say, call it good.

Curiously enough, while I was wringing my hands over missing out on a Christmas tree, there was an interesting development around our garden.

Volunteer firs!

If you're at all familiar with the Foothills of the North Cascades, in the Pacific Northwest, you know that firs and cedars grow like weeds. I can't fathom why I was so surprised, that these trees would eventually turn up in our garden!

You see, over the nearly twenty years we've been here, our originally logged acreage has been recovering. The land, once shorn of its trees, is turning back into a forest. Around the perimeter of our yard and out in the woods, many firs and cedars, especially if they've gotten a fair amount of sunlight, have shot up to beautiful, robust, 30-foot evergreens!

Within our fenced garden, however, these trees have taken root where they are decidedly *not* welcome. Right next to the house foundation, or in the middle of a veggie bed.

Or, like the one I've pre-selected for this year's Christmas, is just two feet away from one of my favorite Chandler blueberry shrubs.

The berry patch's all-day sunlight has been an ideal spot for growing a perfect small tree. Unlike a volunteer in the woods, a sapling that must to scrounge around for light, water, and nutrients, this particular little specimen has been situated to receive all the goodies the blueberries receive: light, lots of water, and nutritious mulch. Now, though only four feet tall, this fast-growing tree is bushy and deep green.

Its roots will very soon—if they haven't already—impact the roots of the neighboring berry shrubs. Clearly, this little four-footer needs to come out. And there's not a better time or purpose than to be this year's Christmas tree. Finally, I can *happily* embrace our simpler tree tradition!

Once it's cut, I'll miss the cheerful sight of that little guy in my garden. Still, this tree will end its days bringing us pleasure. After Epiphany, John will chip it up, and I'll spread the wood chips around my blueberry shrubs, protecting them from the winter cold.

Evergreens may symbolize eternal life, yet here at our little farm, watching our firs grow through the years, I see an age-old cycle in miniature. Tiny sprouts emerging from the clear cut, to maturing fir trees dropping their cones, to new baby trees popping up. The few that we cut will eventually get recycled back to the earth, giving more life to the plants they nourish.

Nature brings her own magic to Christmas.

CHRISTMAS FAIRY MAGIC

"The dreams of childhood…its airy fables, its graceful, beautiful humane, impossible adornments of the world beyond; so good, to be believed in once, so good to be remembered when outgrown." —Charles Dickens

SOMETIMES, holiday magic comes from unexpected places.

If you're familiar with some of my books or my Little Farm blog, you may know I'm a big fairy fan. As in, I *love* fairies.

The first Halloween in my memory, I was thrilled to go trick-or-treating as Flora, the fairy from Disney's "Sleeping Beauty" animated film. I adored my store-bought, sateen gown, and played dress-up in it afterward until it fell apart.

My fairy fondness only grew from there. For many years, I've kept a small treasury of fairy books and fairy figurines in my office. I have a tiny fairy snow globe, and a larger ceramic fairy king—who seems to have a twinkle in his eyes. You may not be surprised that fairy lore makes its way into my writing too.

The room also holds my most prized fairy possession: a

photo of our first granddaughter at age one. A shy smile on her face, she's wearing a little tulle skirt, a sparkly wand in her small hand, with a set of tiny wings on her shoulders.

Well, it seems obvious that I was destined to, someday, write a fairy story. The question was when, and what would actually happen in the story!

In my experience, inspiration for a story can come from anywhere. Or out of nowhere. Often, you have no clue the smallest inkling of an idea can stay in the far recesses of your mind for a really long time—until the story pixies let it loose.

Anyway, one late fall, a few years back, the photo of our baby granddaughter kept drawing my eyes. Although this granddaughter was growing up fast, and long ago had consigned her fairy dress to a storage box, there was something in her baby smile, in the little fairy wings, that tugged even more strongly at my heart.

A story began to take shape in my mind. A kid's chapter book.

I scribbled a few notes, then went straight to my laptop. But I didn't start typing. Instead, I clicked on a colorful illustration I'd been keeping on my hard drive for a couple of years.

The image features a snow-covered landscape with a tree in the center—but it's not just any tree. It's a fairy tree.

A wooden door is set into the trunk, and above it, the tree's rich green limbs droop with snow. Amidst the greenery, there are several little windows, each with a gleam of golden light behind the curtains—and in one of them, there's a wee blue pitcher. An otherworldly pink glow suffuses the scene. It's easy to imagine that this place really *is* a home for fairies.

I would open the jpeg file every once in a while to simply gaze at the photo. Every time I did, I would tell myself, *I'm going to write a story about that fairy tree someday.*

On this particular day, just a couple of weeks from Christmas, I gazed at the image for the longest time, and thought, *Someday has finally come.*

Small problem: I was busy working on another project, a Christmas novel, *The Hopeful Romantic.* And I've always been the kind of writer who can only work on one book at a time.

But I was hit by an overwhelming urge to write my middle-grade fairy book in time for Christmas, come what may. As the story possessed me, all my holiday preparations fell by the wayside. I didn't bake, I didn't write Christmas cards, and my Advent calendar windows went unopened.

I'm a slow writer, and always have been. Yet in an unprecedented writing binge, I banged out my kid's book in six days.

When I came up for air Christmas Eve, I realized I'd written the book so fast it was like there was some powerful force beyond me, helping me bring it to life. I couldn't *not* write it. John proofread the book for me, and within hours, it was ready: *Morgan Carey and The Mystery of the Christmas Fairies*, the story of scrappy 5th grader Morgan, and her adventures in a magical forest. And how she learned what family is truly all about.

But there's another classic Christmas fairy book I'd very much like to tell you about. Just weeks before I'd banged out my fairy chapter book, I had come across an unforgettable holiday story.

A *fairy* story, called *The Wee Christmas Cabin of Carn-na-ween,* an Irish picture book by Ruth Sawyer.

If you read only one holiday picture book this season, I hope it's this one. Despite the story's rather mournful theme, *The Wee Christmas Cabin* has a universality that speaks to readers of all ages—a tender, mystical tale that will stay with you long after you close the cover.

As you'll discover in *The Wee Christmas Cabin,* some things can't be explained.

Like the spirit of fairies.

THE SEASON OF GIVING

The original Christmas story tells us about the gifts of the Magi to the Christ child—and as we all know, it's the reason we celebrate the holidays by exchanging presents. Then came St. Nicholas, evolving over the centuries into Santa Claus or Father Christmas, who embody the spirit of giving and its many blessings.

What's interesting is that scientific research confirms what we probably have sensed already—that giving warms the heart of the *giver*, even more than the recipient!

When it comes to holiday gift-giving, I've traveled a long and winding road...and have ended up not far from where I began.

Compared to modern holiday gift traditions, the Christmases of my childhood were very basic. By today's standards, even Spartan. Yet to me, the holidays felt rich and glorious—the lights and special treats, the Christmas program at school, and, since my siblings and I didn't have a lot of toys, the dizzying prospect of presents!

Through my life, I've often yearned for the simpler gifting traditions of my childhood. You would get one toy (yes, that's *one*), and for me, it was always a doll. My earliest memory was getting a baby doll, the next year a bride doll, then Santa graduated to giving me a Barbie.

My siblings and I would also receive a few do-dads, maybe a pair of mittens, and from the wealthy grandma we seldom saw, we girls would get a pretty new pinafore. With these rare new outfits, my sisters and I were, as the Irish say, thrilled to *bits*.

Really, you may be thinking. *This sounds like the 1880s. Is Susan going to claim she also used to walk 10 miles to school and back in the snow every day, both ways uphill?*

But when I was seven years old, this grandmother I didn't really know very well gave me something even better than a pinafore: a cream-colored fuzzy hat with ringlets knitted into it. As a little girl who had a pixie haircut and *ached* for long curls, I was overcome with joy.

My other grandmother, the Laurence Welk grandma, was a steady presence during my childhood. Although Social Security was her only income, she always gave me and my four siblings several holiday gifts.

She would buy bits and bobs in the small-town dime store, and would wrap each one in plain green or red tissue paper, tied up with curly ribbon—red ribbon for the green packages, and green for the red ones.

To this day, every time I see that classic tissue gift wrap, I think of her…and how her simple presents will always remain a cherished memory. Yet in my life, I received one other precious, unforgettable gift. One that forever lives in my heart.

The Blue Robe

The loveliest gift I've ever received
Is the blue bathrobe you gave me
All those Christmases ago.
You, my sister and first "daughter," just a slip of a girl,

Spent a small fortune at Nordstrom's to buy it.
A delicate pastel, the elegant, fluffy robe was
Warm and comforting and always there for me.
Like you.

ALL THOSE CHRISTMASES AGO,
    We two sisters were mothers together
    Raising two sisters.
    Because of the way you cared for me,
    Looked after me,
    Brought out the best in me,
    I was your first daughter as you were mine.
    The four of us a little tribe of mothers and sisters and daughters,
    A circle of love that began
    With you.

I LOUNGED in the robe each morning,
    Snuggled in it with my girls at night,
    And before I climbed into bed,
    Draped the robe on top of my bedspread.
    Although you weren't there,
    I felt warm and comforted.

THEN LIFE CHANGED.
    To a no-lounging life.
    The days were too full, the nights too rushed
    To cuddle in fluffy terrycloth.
    But still, the blue bathrobe hung in my closet,
    Reminding me of you,
    Waiting patiently.

Patient. Like you.

THE YEARS WENT BY.
>   Every once in a while I'd take out
>   The blue robe,
>   Put it through the wash and think,
>   I'd like to lounge again, wearing this.
>   But life had expanded.
>   A larger garden, a larger family, larger responsibilities.
>   When would I lounge?

ALL THOSE CHRISTMASES ago
>   Became a quarter-century.
>   Despite washing, the elegant robe had
>   A faint rust stain around the neckline, and
>   More stains down the front.
>   It had grown faded and careworn,
>   Like the face I saw in the mirror.
>   I worked outside in shabby, stained garments
>   I wouldn't wear them at night too.

EVERY ONCE IN A WHILE,
>   I'd go through my closet,
>   Culling items to donate.
>   Garments I'd stopped wearing, would never wear again.
>   I would eye the blue bathrobe, but then
>   I would be reminded of you,
>   And the circle of love we four girls had made.
>   I could not bring myself to give it away.

. . .

SUSAN COLLEEN BROWNE

U NTIL THIS WEEK.

A PHOTOGRAPH in the Sunday paper
    Showed a New York City policeman, on a frigid night
    Kneeling at the bare, dirty feet of a homeless man, offering the
    Boots the cop had bought for him,
    One of the nameless, unloved, discarded.
    The cop so like the man whose birthday we celebrate at Christmas,
    Who once knelt to the nameless, unloved, discarded
    To wash their bare, dirty feet.
    How could I keep the blue robe another quarter-century, when some
    Cold, distressed person could wear it on a frigid night
    And feel warm and comforted?

SO THIS WEEK,
    I found a clear plastic bag for the items I'd chosen
    To donate.
    I touched the soft, comforting nap of the blue robe once last time,
    Then resolutely slung it off its hanger,
    Bundled it up,
    And stuffed it at the bottom of the bag.

I WALKED into the Salvation Army store
    Cradling the clear plastic bag in my arms,
    Heading straight for the donation bin.
    Maybe someone who really needs a robe could
    Be wearing this tonight, I thought.

Quickly setting the bag in the bin,
I turned to leave, and my eyes caught
Once last flash of pastel blue.

Soon I was outside, the merest wisp of snow,
    Like a frozen mist, was cold on my face.
    An icy flake blew into my eyes,
    Stinging like tears.
    I thought of you, and the circle we had created.
    Regretting that the bonds of sisters and mothers and daughters
    Had grown fragile and tenuous.

Still, as I gaze outside on this December day
    At the gently falling snow, I'm reminded of
    All those Christmases ago,
    And the circle that will always
    Begin and end at the same place.
    With you.

CELEBRATIONS OF LIGHT

*S*eeking light in the depths of winter surely must be universal.

The Irish in antiquity were so attuned to wonder and light that they built a tomb, Newgrange, with an intricate, extraordinary design. At the tomb, sunlight penetrates into a special passage and illuminates an inner chamber—but *only* at the time of the winter solstice.

In the Northern Hemisphere, the solstice and celebrating light at Christmastime seem intertwined. Throughout the ages, the return of light, of life-giving sunshine has been a gift—a reason to rejoice!

I know folks who set aside a day to observe the solstice with a special gathering. Living in the Pacific Northwest at the 49th Parallel, where it gets dark by 3:30 pm in December, John and I especially look forward to the solstice. We always feel a fresh sense of gratitude, to think of more light on its way, each day bringing the blessing of few more minutes of daylight.

Hanukkah brings yet more light to the winter holidays. I find this holiday's rituals quite lovely, not just because some very special people we know celebrate it, but for the way the candle-lighting and blessings extend over eight days.

Light-centered celebrations, through the years, have come to mean even more to John and me. Because there were so many days during the winter holiday season, when we didn't have any light at all.

One December, just before Christmas Eve, the forecast was for epic rainfall—and we got a snowstorm instead. An unexpected snowfall at our place often brings concern, and this one, so close to Christmas, was no exception.

My anxiety mounted as the Internet went out first, then the power. As the inches accumulated, a cottonwood tree bent sideways over our narrow private lane, blocking access to the outside world. I had to cancel a needed trip to town—not quite a hardship—yet the soon-to-arrive Northeaster system was far more worrying. And as it so often does, that strong Northeast wind extended the power outage for another 24 hours.

The following day, after the power was restored, I brought out the DVD of a popular television series I enjoyed. This show follows a family through the decades, and even into the future. While this family's experiences were always ultimately life-affirming, the series didn't shy away from illness or hardship or even tragedy.

The episode I watched turned out to be an especially heartrending one, centered around one of the sons and his long-estranged biological father at the end of his life.

There was a moment when the younger man gently held his dying father's face between his hands. The older man was frightened of what was to come, but his son just held him, telling him to *breathe*.

Watching the son's tenderness, I felt my tension ease. Wrapped in an afghan, the Christmas tree lights glowing nearby, I was also reminded of how small my worries were. Whether you're focusing on everyday troubles, or your heart is breaking, you can take a moment and do the same. Simply *breathe*.

Or when holiday stresses with family or finances or trying to do way too much gets overwhelming, you can do the same. Just breathe.

Give yourself a little understanding. A little tenderness. And take another slow, easy breath.

In that pause, you might notice small wonders. They say the devil's in the details, but perhaps it's the *divine* that is in the details—like the slanting winter sun through the trees, the kindness in your neighbor's face, the gleam of a meteor shooting through the midnight sky.

Even if you generally give traditional winter holidays a pass, surely the end of the darkest days of the season, the beginning of longer daylight hours is worth paying attention to.

Fortunately, snowstorms or holiday stress, whatever it is, shall pass. So, as darkness falls on these chilly December nights, I hope you can put your mind and spirit on pause, and take in the marvels around you.

THE SEASON OF SHOPPING

When it comes to the holidays, despite the wonder and magic and spirit of giving, there's no avoiding the big contradiction…

It's inherent in the story of my blue robe, purchased by a loving sister despite her small income. The thing is, you can't really think about the marvels of Christmas without the practical aspect. To wit: money.

In the years John and I have been pursuing a simpler life, my daughters have started their own families, and their own holiday traditions. Over time, without the kids' expectations, we've created Christmas celebrations where gifts are an afterthought, not the main event. But it wasn't always this way.

Far from it.

Back in the day, when I was married to my first husband and my two girls were young, I spent the weeks preceding Christmas in a flurry of mall-visits. I'd frantically search Toys-R-Us for the perfect Cabbage Patch doll or My Little Pony, schlepping around overflowing bags until my arms ached.

Then came the real challenge: trying to find hiding places for all that booty!

When the girls got older, I trolled the aisles of Bon Marche, seeking that perfect sweater or the most fashionable jeans. Then it was off to the big-box stores to select only the most gorgeous wrapping paper, ribbons and bows. All these shopping trips would culminate in a post-midnight wrap-a-thon late Christmas Eve night—often till two a.m. or later.

Christmas morning, I'd be so wiped out I could hardly enjoy the kids' present-opening. But I had zero downtime—there was our big turkey dinner to prepare! Knowing how utterly exhausting the whole drill was going to be, no wonder I approached the holidays with some level of dread.

Some years later, I met a kindred spirit in John. He approached Christmas with the sense of wonder and quiet joy I hadn't felt since childhood. Our one problem: he and I ended up "celebrating" Christmas all year long. That is, we bought so many holiday gifts that it took us the next twelve months to pay off our credit cards.

Starting our lives together, John and I lived in what we now call "town," the mid-sized city where we got married and worked and bought a house. But when he and I conceived a dream to start a homestead in the country, we needed to save every dime. Finally, we had no choice but to stop running up our credit cards.

You may wonder: after lavishly buying Christmas gifts for many years of my life, how did I make a change toward simpler giving? How does a person actually jump off the spending merry-go-round, without wrecking the holidays?

It didn't happen in one fell swoop.

Changing my holiday habits took me years of soul-searching. With all my reading and pondering and researching, I was deeply inspired by other people who had somehow managed to downsize Christmas. During this time, I was teaching a lot of creativity workshops—and discovered that creativity actually dovetailed quite a bit with this holiday downsizing idea.

Even after immersing myself in this entirely new mindset, I also had to give myself lots of pep talks. To be honest, I was dealing with the inevitable apprehension... *How will the people in my life handle the new minimal-gifting me? Will they think I'm cheap?*

Yet it was more than *telling* myself that Christmas isn't about gifts, it's about peace and optimism. I had to get to a place where I felt it in my heart.

JINGLE ALL THE WAY...

"*O*h, for the good old days, when people would stop Christmas shopping when they ran out of money." — Author Unknown

AS I SAID, the new, low-impact gifting mindset I'd developed did come with new worries. You might have them too: *Giving (my loved one) a smaller gift than last year, will they think I don't love them as much?* And spending less, I also stressed over the eternal Christmas question: *Is this present good enough?*

But there's something about being really intentional about what you buy that brings a different kind of peace to the holidays.

No matter what your financial situation is, very few of us can resist the immense, modern holiday industry, the advertising and marketing, the siren song of *buy, buy, buy*. The "shoulds" of giving. It seems that Christmas is all about "jingles"—as long as the jingling is the coins you're using to buy gifts!

Which makes me wonder, how did creating a joyful holiday

become associated with money? As in, the more you spend, the happier your Christmas will be?

Of course I'm not the first to wonder about all this, to mourn the fact that gifts and celebrations keep getting more expensive and extravagant, and the expectations for them keep growing. I always figured this had developed over the last 30 years or so.

Then I came across some holiday musings in the 1910 novel *Howards End*, by author E.M. Forster.

"...Peace? It may bring other gifts, but is there a single Londoner to whom Christmas is peaceful? The craving for excitement and for elaboration has ruined that blessing..."

The longing for a simpler holiday then, is nothing new.

Given how much John and I transformed our lives—even ourselves—to start our homestead, it's not surprising that the experience changed our gifting forever. Once we started living a good distance from the city we'd left, a vibrant community full of entertainment and cultural opportunities, we were fully immersed in creating our homestead, developing our garden, and adjusting to this absorbing new life.

Naturally, John and I spent less and less time in "town." We still made the trip for grocery runs, doctor appointments, and seeing friends. But visits to the mall or to the movie theatre dwindled, then stopped entirely. The same goes for restaurant meals. Which worked out for us, because the city, over the years, had turned into an expensive, traffic-clogged, sprawling commercial center.

As the years passed, John and I developed an increasingly practical, homesteady outlook. Spending on frou-frou items went out the window, particularly when it came to holiday gifts. We've always been of modest means, so it made good sense to gear our spending toward useful, everyday items: garden tools and homestead equipment, warm gloves, socks and flannel sheets.

As we avoided shopping more and more, I was amazed how much money we could save by simply not going into stores!

Then along came shopping on the internet, with its ease and convenience. Sure, it helped John and me save time and gas *and* aggravation going into town—and continues to do so. But looking at the bigger picture, I really regret what online shopping has done to the holidays.

Do you wonder how—or maybe more importantly, *why*—the Christmas season has started booting up in October? Christmas decorations, Christmas candy, Christmas ads, Christmas books and Christmas movies? I've been giving it some thought.

These days, as screens dominate our daily routines, maybe we're yearning for something *real*. Perhaps our senses are starved for more light and color and tactile experiences: the scents of fir and spices, the comfort of warm, fuzzy sweaters, the coziness of candle flames and a blaze in the fireplace.

Maybe we're also craving special foods that aren't just a styled photo seen online, but a much-loved dish we're taking the care and trouble to make. No wonder so many of us can't wait for the annual holiday feast of the senses!

WHATEVER THE REASON for the early start to the season, I guess it's a lucky thing Thanksgiving is still sandwiched in there somehow.

Can anyone remember what it was like when Thanksgiving was its own holiday? You didn't mind cooking for two or even three days straight, because a grand feast felt rare and wonderful, and a day dedicated to being thankful made it even more so. Plus all through that weekend, you could loll around eating turkey sandwiches and leftover pumpkin pie. There were no other expectations.

I used to anticipate Thanksgiving because I would see my

parents and siblings. And because Advent was just around the corner. And definitely for the food.

Now Thanksgiving, and for several days before and after, is all about online shopping. Essentially, *sales*! Pre-Black Friday/Black Friday/Black Friday Weekend deals. Yet there's more—Cyber Monday sales!

I understand that during these days, retail websites are hardly able to keep up without crashing. And I'm fairly certain that people who still try to go online on from Thanksgiving Friday through Monday encounter a lot of delays or frozen web pages.

Then there's "Giving Tuesday." Now, don't get me wrong. Designating a day for helping those in need and worthy causes is absolutely lovely. Or it would be, if so many retailers didn't find a way to simply extend the Black Friday deals all the way through that day as well.

I'm not quite sure how uber-commercialism crept into a holiday that was meant to be about gratitude. I'm guessing it's kind of like the frog in the pot of heating water: little by little, that poor critter got more and more uncomfortable until, before you know it, the situation hit the boiling point and that frog was a goner.

Also, "Black Friday" sounds just grim to me, in a medieval kind of way. Like the *end* of something (like the frog, for example), instead of the *beginning* of the Christmas season. As far as I'm concerned, clicking and waiting in front of ad-laden screens in hopes of scoring that big sale is a dismal way of spending one's precious time off.

I know, I'm really on my soapbox here. Yet it feels like this end-of-November craze of more and more online buying, and living in front of a screen can't end well.

Maybe, the way things are going, with more folks simultaneously shopping and checking social media for the best products, pretty soon the entire Internet—six days from Thanksgiving through the following Tuesday—will go the way of that poor frog: dead in the water.

I'm also well aware that by suggesting that everyone avoids the whole Black Friday thing, I'm swimming against the tide. Or trying to resist an extremely strong undertow. Still, I want to try... So, how can we restore Thanksgiving to its original meaning?

I propose something *radical*...

A SEASON OF THANKS

What if everyone decided to rebel? Ignore all the Black Friday deals and come-ons, the opportunities to save *big*, and stop shopping altogether, from Thanksgiving into the next week? If you celebrate Thanksgiving, to turn your November holiday into something very different from the current shopping spree?

If you're game to go cold-turkey on the TG week shop-a-thon, life awaits!

Now, as a workshop teacher, I'm in the habit and sharing "how to's." How to grow a homestead garden. How to write your memoir. I even taught a class about "How to simplify your holidays."

As an instructor, it's my job to provide suggestions. So I hope you won't mind this one for changing up Thanksgiving:

Instead of shopping, there's the great outdoors to be thankful for and enjoy! (Weather and abilities permitting.) Indoors, how about board games, crossword puzzles, crafts, building a blanket fort? For gardeners, there's planning next year's garden, and looking through last year's seed catalogues before the new ones come in.

As a book lover, I'm lobbying for something that you can do at home, is easy *and* it's inexpensive or even free: a book celebration!

How about swapping out shopping for *reading*...and you can spend your Thanksgiving weekend curling up with a book. (Or books!) And being thankful for the gift of reading!

Here are some tips for reading more books:

*Put your phone in another room. While you're at it, you might as well turn off your notifications.

*If possible, go for a *physical* book—something you can hold, and it's time away from screens. And if the book belongs to you, you can underline the good stuff, write notes in it, or even doodle in the margins!

*Keep a book with you when you leave the house—for those moments you're waiting in line, or for appointments.

*Don't push yourself to read more than you feel like—maybe just five or ten pages at a time.

*Read something *you* enjoy—that lightens your spirit, delivers a thrill, or gives you that "Calgon, take me away" feeling...i.e., pure escapism.

*Comic books, graphic novels, and books you loved as a child all count. You don't have to choose something you feel you *ought* to read.

*Audiobooks count too!

(Thank you to *The Guardian* for the inspiration, and their article, "How to put your phone down and get back into the habit of reading books," October 11, 2024)

For this weekend read-fest, in the week(s) before Thanksgiving, all you need to do is line up some books...borrow, buy, or put books on hold at your local public library.

Once you dive into a read, regular breaks are good even for the most avid readers. Getting out of our heads, and doing something tactile or physical, or just hanging out with your peeps for a while is a treat for the mind, body and spirit. (The motto from my days working at the YMCA.)

Our dear neighbors celebrate Thanksgiving the conventional way—with food, family and friends. But they've designated the day after as "Friday Pie Day." An idea I absolutely love. They keep it super simple: they prepare extra apple/pumpkin/mincemeat pies—enough for a second gathering—then for Friday, bring in take-out pizza (pie). Voila! Friday Pie Day!

I'd like to rename the whole shebang to "Gratitude Weekend," or maybe "Thankful Week." Like every year, John and I won't be shopping over Thanksgiving, and this year, we've been invited to the Friday Pie Day party. Nothing to buy except ingredients for a dish to pass.

It may not make sense, but John and I (as I said, our income is pretty modest) would rather pay more for an item, then spend our precious life's energy Thanksgiving weekend trying to save money. It's certainly the reason he and I will never be wealthy!

But living in the middle of a peaceful woods, and knowing I wouldn't want to live anywhere else—or any *way* else—I feel rich in every way.

BETTER THAN PRESENTS

I admit, even living where some people call "out in the middle of nowhere," there's no escaping the commercial frenzy of modern Christmases.

Catalogs jamming your mailbox… overpriced gift suggestions filling your favorite magazines…the social pressure to come up with something for everyone you know…the flood of seasonal movies that depict a perfect holiday…

It's difficult to avoid it, sure. But not impossible.

I spent many years slowly working on my gifting self-acceptance, and making what felt like hard choices, yet there was something else that really helped me get off the holiday-spending bullet train—to see our modern Christmas commercialism a little more clearly.

It's the holiday rituals of other countries. Your time and attention is all that's needed, not present-buying. Oh, wait: there's cooking and eating yummy food too.

In Sweden, the Christmas season begins December 13th, when Swedes celebrate the feast day of Saint Lucia. Originally, it was the winter solstice celebration, since the date coincided with the solstice on the Julian calendar from antiquity.

It was believed that evil spirits were out and about on Solstice night, so you needed to keep alert. And what better way to stay awake than to turn up the lights (candles) and eat delicious treats!

These beliefs evolved into a new tradition: young girls would wear an evergreen wreath with seven lighted candles upon their heads, and serve their families coffee and buns.

The magic seems to be that not many girls' hair has caught on fire! (Or else someone would have surely come up with a new way to celebrate.) I understand that in Sweden, St. Lucia's day has become a big deal: parades are held, and the stars of the show are girls in white dresses, holding candles and evergreens.

One family I'm acquainted with really does have the youngest daughter wake up the rest of the family, wearing a crown and bringing them buns!

Light and warmth figures strongly in other Scandinavian traditions too, like the Finnish ritual of burning a gigantic Yule Log. Light is also a feature of German holiday traditions—Advent candles (and calendars) originated in Germany.

You might also like the Christmas rituals of Switzerland—apparently there's lots of bell ringing, and people feast on huge homemade doughnuts called *ringli*.

Maybe it's the Danish who seem to truly embody the holiday spirit of *love*—giving each other baskets made from paper hearts filled with candy.

And the French custom of *le réveillon*, a big family meal that takes place after midnight Mass on Christmas Eve, must be really splendid (or magical)—since everyone of all ages seems to have the energy to stay awake for the big celebration. What I admire about all of these rituals is the spirit of community and sharing.

. . .

Yet when it comes to holiday magic and whimsy, I think the traditions of Iceland are the most intriguing—although these rituals go a little against the typical holiday grain…they're not all Christmasy light and love. From what I can tell, Icelandic people have a reputation for dwelling on the dark side.

But can you blame them? My mother, a sociology professor and worldwide traveler, journeyed extensively around Iceland a couple of years ago. She said, "it's the grimmest land mass of any country I've ever seen—miles and miles of uninhabitable land. It takes a special people to live there."

I suppose when you live in such an isolated, chilly environment, with volcanoes in your back yard and winters that seem mostly night-time, maybe it makes sense to celebrate Christmas with a bit of dark humor. In this case, it's the Icelandic legend of the Yule Lads.

Starting December 12th until Christmas, children in Iceland would traditionally leave a shoe in the windowsill each night, and wait for the Yule Lads' visit. The Lads are the 13 sons of mountain trolls who creep down from their rugged wilderness to visit the towns and villages across Iceland. And if you've been good, a Yule Lad will leave a sweet or gift in your shoe.

Now this all sounds quite benevolent, doesn't it? However, the Lads' true purpose is to make mischief, do pranks, and pretty much wreak havoc on people's houses.

Each of the 13 trolls has a name that relates to his own brand of prank—think "Bowl Licker" or "Sausage Swiper." *And* each troll gets his very own night to make trouble, in the 13 nights leading up to Christmas. That's in *addition* to what happens to naughty kids: you won't get candy, not even a lump of coal like Santa leaves for the baddies…you get a rotten potato.

Being a food gardener, I have encountered many a decomposed, nasty potato in my vegetable beds—so trust me, a rotten spud is far worse than coal. In any event, as the Lads' visitations begin, you'll have to be on your guard lest those wily trolls ruin your holidays…

The first troll night, December 12th, watch out for "Sheep-Cote Clod." His goal is to sneak into your shed and harass your sheep. I'm sure you've barely gotten your flock settled down and your ewes milked before the next Lad arrives…

December 13th, along comes "Gully Gawk," who slurps the foam off the milk in your bucket. By now, your sheep are likely thoroughly rattled, but you're in luck. The following Lads begin a series of raids on the *inside* of Icelandic homes.

The next Lad, the night of the 14th, is "Stubby." He's the shortest of the bunch, but judging from his picture, he seems to be the jolliest one. In his quest to steal bits of food from frying pans, he's probably happy that he's first in line to scarf up the kitchen goodies.

On December 15th, it's "Spoon-Licker's" night—he goes after the spoons used to scrape food from pots and pans. How convenient, then, that December 16th, along comes "Pot Scraper" to continue to job, eating the food anyone is negligent enough to leave in the pots.

The 17th is the night for "Bowl Licker," to (obviously) lick all the inside of the bowls used for mixing food. Apparently he has zero discrimination, since he even goes for the pets' bowls.

By now, your house is likely quite topsy-turvy—so you'll be glad to hear that December 18th, there's a little break from all the food-stealing… "Door-Slammer" arrives to disrupt the holiday peace, banging doors all through the night. I imagine he's scaring the sheep too.

Before we get to the 19th …

When it comes to entertainment, I'm all for the lighter side of the holidays…no movies like "Bad Santa" or "The Nightmare Before Christmas" for me. When it comes to the Yule Lads, I understand they are more pranksters and mischief-makers, rather than out-and-out *bad*.

I'm actually surprised they turned out so well, considering their mother…

Grŷla, who's responsible for these 13 annoying trolls, is a troll as well…and actually *evil*. Back in the day, she was the means by which Icelandic parents controlled wayward kiddos. In fact, parents would let their children know that if they misbehaved, Grŷla could come and abduct them!

If you're after social control, Grŷla sounds far more effective than what the Yule Lads could dish out with the rotten potato. But her legend seems far too dark for me, so let's focus back on her offspring.

December 19th brings back yet another food-obsessed Yule Lad, "Skyr-Gobbler." He's the one who devours the Icelandic yogurt-like dairy product. December 20th, "Sausage-Swiper" arrives. He hides out in the rafters of houses where meat is smoked, and grabs sausages whenever he can.

I think we can all agree that the Lad for the 21st is pretty creepy: "Window-Peeper." He peers through windows to check out whatever stuff is worth stealing.

You may wonder, with all this bad behavior—nothing but trouble-making since the 12th of December—where the heck is the Yule Lads' father? And why doesn't he take them in hand?

Well, legend has it that Leppalûōi, their dad, isn't quite evil, like his wife Grŷla—just lazy. Apparently not into parenting either. Looks like Grŷla can't use that time-honored stratagem, "You guys are going to get it when your father comes home!"

Too bad, because we have three more nights of troll mayhem and pranks.

Although being trolls, all the Lads have oversized, unattractive noses, December 22nd brings the Lad with the biggest: "Doorway Sniffer." Since he loves to smell baked goods, he uses that big schnozz to stand in doorways, sniffing out any cakes and the Icelandic specialty lacebread he can abscond with.

On December 23rd, another hungry troll, "Meat Hook," arrives with a pole—and a hook at the end. He hovers near the kitchen, and when the cook isn't looking, he'll hook the meat from the pan.

Interestingly, the Scandinavian feature of seeking light coincides with the last Yule Lad's visit, "Candle Beggar." On Christmas Eve, this lover of candles may be the biggest killjoy of all. On this holy night, the night of light and celebration, he will try to sneak off with any unattended candle he finds.

It could be that by Christmas, the Lads have pretty well cleaned out all the food in Icelandic households. So it seems especially unfair that misbehaving kids get spoiled taters, but the Yule Lads' naughtiness goes unpunished!

Now, this tradition does sound all a bit outlandish, right? Surely, no one pays attention to the Yule Lad myths anymore?

Well, it appears that they do. My mom observed that "a number of Icelanders actually believe in trolls and elves and the entire business. They put out food and other items to ease their 'lives.'" Although rural people, she understood, go for these legends more than urban.

Mom also said she wasn't sure if it was a Santa Claus thing or something else, but Iceland's literature is apparently full of these make-believe creatures.

I find the Yule Lads quite wonderfully reminiscent of Middle Earth/Lord of the Rings—and an entirely fresh spin on the holidays. But if you want to go full-on with the troll/dark vibe, you should know Iceland also has the myth of the Yule Cat.

Parents have been using Santa as a way to influence behavior since forever…but the Yule Cat is a whole different approach. It's a terrifying monster meant to scare kids into being good.

Personally, though I find the Lads entertaining, I draw the line at the Yule Cat.

But the Lads may have a deeper wisdom to offer. The holidays aren't meant to be a Hallmark movie, all eggnog in frosted mugs, a perfectly decorated tree, and well-behaved people. Christmas can be full of the chaos of life—like the Lads' mischief-making. Maybe their message is, that despite the messiness, to make a little room for joy.

If you're interested in getting a look at the Yule Lads, you'll find illustrations of all 13 pranksters on my Little Farm in the Foothills blog, or you can check out the official Iceland website.

While Yule Lads are all about myth, I adore the more down-to-earth Icelandic celebration of "Jolabokaflod"—a rough translation is "Christmas book flood." People give books as gifts. And on Christmas Eve, the lucky recipients spend the evening reading and drinking hot chocolate, preferably in front of the fire.

Sounds like heaven. And if you have time for a post-holiday book-reading binge, "Jolabokaflod" is surely the icing on your Christmas cake.

ICELAND'S YULE LADS, in that cold, often grim country, certainly bring out the lighter side of holiday myths. Traveling south to sunny Italy, a Christmas tradition turns deeply poignant.

The Italian legend tells us that when the Three Wise Men were traveling to see Baby Jesus, they passed La Befana, the Good Witch, busy sweeping and cleaning. The Wise Men pressed her to join them, but she would not leave her chores. They had to depart without her.

After the Wise Men departed, she suddenly changed her mind. But it was too late. Now, La Befana spends Christmas Eve wandering, in search of the Christ Child, whom she never finds.

So in every home, she leaves gifts for each child, who is "holy" in her eyes.

What speaks to me about Befana is her love and longing—the yearning for what can never be. That too, is part of Christmas—the hope of recapturing one's childhood hopes and fantasies and knowing it's not possible. Yet hoping all the same.

BLEAK HOLIDAY

The stories in this little book may give you impression that the holiday season should be pretty much all sweetness and light. After all, so many of us wish and long for—and even fantasize about—that rosy glow you find in a Hallmark holiday film. I've wished for it myself.

Of having a merry, *perfect* Christmas.

But we all have hard times—definitely un-jolly and un-merry periods of our lives. And those times can inconveniently happen around the holidays.

There was a Christmas not so long ago when a crisis in our family was breaking my heart. On the days leading up to that sad and difficult holiday—and for many days after—I couldn't see any of the light I yearned for. Or the gift of peace Christmas can bring.

The situation has since resolved, thank goodness, and that little family and their lives have been steadily moving in a positive direction. Yet I can't approach the holidays now without remembering that heartbreak.

Just as I still remember, after all these years, the young Ukrainian family at the post office. Since the mother didn't have even $28 in her bank account, I imagine she and her kids had a bleak holiday that year. I can only hope wherever they are, Christmas this year is better.

But as I said, you don't always get to *choose* a merry holiday. Some years back, John and I had months on end of difficulties and heartbreak. For a long while, I couldn't imagine feeling peace or a sense of rightness again.

Garrison Keillor says being joyful is a large task for people from the Midwest, "where our idea of a compliment is, 'It could have been worse.'"

But when it comes to that awful year, I sometimes think that it actually *couldn't*.

THIS PARTICULAR YEAR had been one of many sorrows and challenges—and surely any truthful account of it would be too disheartening to revisit, much less share. Still, here I am.

That difficult year began even before January first. The holiday season promised to be already sad—John and I were facing our first Christmas after his mother passed away. His childhood home had just been sold too—the place where he'd grown up, where he'd brought his kids for family holidays, where his parents had lived for 50 years—and he was grieving over the loss.

On New Year's Eve, I was cooking dinner when we found a voicemail on the phone—from a hospital in Phoenix, Arizona.

John's son lived there.

He had been in a car accident, hit by a distracted driver. My stepson's injuries were serious; after extensive surgeries, he was in no shape to care for himself. John spent six weeks in Phoenix looking after him.

It was a lonely time for me—worried for my stepson, and trying to look after our homestead by myself in the darkest days of winter. It's true that with John away, I learned to be more self-sufficient—yet I also got a taste of what widowhood might feel like.

John's return and the advent of spring was a lift. But the day after he got back, we got another phone call. It was John's brother—their sister's cancer had progressed and she had only a few weeks to live.

As it turned out, the time she had left was only days. Right away, we traveled to her care center on the other side of the state to say a final goodbye. She died two days after our visit. Losing her felt all the more poignant knowing she had struggled through illness for much of her life. And that she, who had such a generous and loving heart, and who adored kids, never had children of her own.

Two months later...John's birthday begins one of the loveliest months of the year in the Foothills—the sun doesn't set until 10 o'clock. But the day I baked him a birthday cake, we faced a plague of tent caterpillars—a plague of such Biblical proportions we could never have imagined it. So it began, our month-long battle: we hand-killed caterpillars up to eight hours a day to save our orchard and berry plants.

The plague cycle finally worked its way out; the caterpillars died back. Still, I felt like I'd lost one precious month of my life.

John and I were just regrouping when we had another loss: our small flock of chickens was killed by a cougar. For the first time since we moved here, I wanted to get away from our place. Get away from the sad little corpses, from the feathers strewn around the chicken run, from the empty coop. Get away from the guilt we both felt—that we'd let our girls down by not protecting them.

After so many blows this year, after this one, I couldn't seem to bounce back.

There's a verse in the Old Testament that has become part of the Christmas story: "The people who walked in darkness have seen a great light."

Looking back, I can see that it was the light that brought healing. Six weeks after we lost our chickens, I went to the Pacific Ocean coast with three of our grandchildren. At the beach one evening, I watched the setting sun and the silhouette of my granddaughter frolicking in the surf, and saw the golden-pink light bathing my grandsons' rapt faces as they played in the sand.

I felt an incandescent joy I hadn't experienced in a long time.

In November, John and I traveled to California to see his daughter and family—my first visit to her home. Warmed by the kids' bright little faces, being called Grandma by the children for the first time, walking on the beach in the sunshine, when at home it would be dark and cold, I felt my heart lift even more.

A few days later, John and I took our granddaughter to attend a big-city symphony orchestra—a concert featuring a young singing prodigy. Christmas lights were everywhere—the eighty-foot fir tree in the city center brought back the wonder of my childhood. At the performance of gorgeous music, I feasted my gaze on the stage lights playing on this young artist's face as she sang, the sequins on her gown sparkling, and the vibrant lighting behind the orchestra dancing in the changing hues of a rainbow. It was a transcendent evening.

So after the darkness, if you're patient, the light comes back to you. In December, the holiday month may be the darkest days of the year, but if we can seek the light... The light and hope of the Christmas story, that speaks of a bright star that shone over a miracle, the light of generosity that the season brings.

Sometimes you can create your *own* light. Years ago, John and I experienced a Christmas Day when a storm had knocked the power out, and the snowy roads kept us housebound. It sure didn't feel festive, with the dark Christmas tree, and no holiday meal—only leftovers heated on top of the woodstove.

But as dusk fell, John and I sat together, the woodstove

flames our only light, and exchanged holiday memories from our childhoods. And that seemingly bleak holiday didn't seem so dark and cheerless after all. That night, a quiet joy suffused me—as it does even now, as I recall that night.

In the midst of Christmastime sadness or challenges, I try to take comfort from simple things—a cozy fire in the woodstove, my favorite holiday decorations, rereading the eternal Christmas story from the Bible…

All of which makes me believe the light will always return.

TRAVELING THROUGH TIME

I revisit the Christmases of long ago, to discover that the dreams of childhood, as Charles Dickens says, are so good to be remembered. Years later, you may still feel their magic...

The Ghosts of Christmas Past

FIVE YEARS YOUNG.

Speechless in wonder, gazing at the plate glass windows of Dayton's department store in Minneapolis.

Behind the glass are no motionless mannequins in the latest fashions; these windows are filled with holiday scenes, like a living fairy tale

Dolls in Victorian dress, almost my size, who blink, lifting their arms and nodding their heads like magic.

Despite the cold, I can't tear my eyes away.

. . .

I could've stayed there forever. But there's more wonder awaiting me.

Dad has driven our whole family sixty-five miles to the big city, with something else in mind. We four kids will sit on Santa's lap and have our picture taken.

Then another Christmas comes around, another visit to Dayton's

To ride a mini-train through an indoor Christmas wonderland of "snow" and glitter

And fairy lights,

Elves half-hidden in the mounds of white. I can still see the snowy scene, and feel the enchantment.

The years of believing blend together, scenes in my mind flowing one into the next.

At home. Christmas Eve. I'm curled up next to the grandmother I adore, on the old rec room couch,

Feeling utterly safe and loved, watching Mitch Miller and Lawrence Welk, Grandma's favorite shows. The sweet contraltos of the Lennon Sisters blend together for "White Christmas," when Mom and Dad call from upstairs.

"Come up! Santa's been here!"

I race up the stairs to find a blond bride doll for me, the size of the dolls in the store window. Oh, I believed!

I didn't hear Santa come, but of course he did! How else would the doll in the lacy white gown

Appear under the tree?

Another Christmas. Our aunt in Toronto has sent a package:

Inside is a gigantic Christmas stocking for each of us, handmade of felt, trimmed with gold ribbon and rick-rack.

Mine is red, with "S-u-s-i-e" in green felt letters sewn across the top.

Imagine, my very own, specially-made Christmas stocking!

And that's not all. My eyes widen to find an Advent calendar too, the first one I've ever seen. Christmas images adorned with sparkles. My heart sparks too.

I glow with pleasure, taking turns with my sisters and brother each day,

Opening up a tiny window to reveal a magical Christmas scene.

EIGHT YEARS OLD. The last Christmas I believed.

I awaken to find a small, slim doll with a perfect blond beehive hairdo

Next to my red "Susie" stocking.

My first Barbie!

Then my Christmas memories fade and turn to black, like turning off a TV.

Leaving only a tiny dot of light in the middle of the screen.

CHRISTMAS EVE, a lifetime later. I'm sewing by lamplight

In a shabby single-wide next to a bare, wind-swept cornfield. It's past midnight,

But I'm staying up late to finish my baby's red felt stocking before Christmas morning.

I take the last stitch, hold up the stocking to admire. It's decorated with gold rick-rack and tiny bells

With a name, cut from green felt, sewn across the top. My baby girl's name.

. . .

THE DOT EXPANDS TO LIGHT. I sense the magic again. It's her turn to believe.

CHRISTMAS EVE, two years later. I'm sewing by lamplight
  In the chilly back bedroom of my in-laws' home, next to a bare, wind-swept cornfield
  Two thousand miles from that shabby trailer.
  It's past midnight,
  But I'm staying up late to finish my second baby's red felt stocking before Christmas morning.
  I take the last stitch, hold up the stocking to admire. It's decorated with green sequins and tiny bells
  With a name, cut from green felt, sewn across the top. My newborn baby girl's name.

THE DOT EXPANDS TO LIGHT. The magic returns. It's her turn to believe.

EXTENDING THE HOLIDAY JOY

"*E*ven at Christmas, I long for Christmas." —Beth Kempton

SEEKING joy at Christmas surely part of its magic. Remembering the awe you felt as a child, surely it's natural that you long to feel it again. Or perhaps, as I do, you can't help yearning for a bit of transcendence.

And yet, it's inevitable. The end of Christmas Day.

Does this sound familiar? It was a nice enough Christmas. The usual. You've been so busy the last weeks have been a blur. Now the holiday is over, and you never got to experience the Christmas spirit you'd hoped for. Not even a bit of a Hallmark rosy glow.

All the sparkle and celebrating is over, everyone's tired, and all that's left is cleaning up. True, New Year's Eve is only one week away, but the special anticipation and mystery of Christmas is over.

But to paraphrase Mr. Rogers: *at the end of something there's always the beginning of something else.* As Christmas Day winds down, the holiday doesn't need to end at 12:01 am, December 26th. You can ease into another tradition, as featured in the old carol about the partridge in the pear tree: the Twelve Days of Christmas!

These Twelve Days aren't the ones leading up to Christmas, like with the Icelandic Yule Lads. They start on Christmas Day, and go into early January.

Okay, in our modern times, this stretch of twelve days is no longer all about partridges or pear trees or golden rings or maids a'milking. But why not extend your celebrations with something fresh?

After Christmas, for the next couple of weeks, you can still play holiday music, bake a batch of holiday cookies, or reflect on the meaning of the holidays—anything you didn't get to earlier. The Twelve Days go all the way through Twelfth Night, January 5th, and soon it's The Feast of the Epiphany, January 6th —the day, as legend has it, that the Three Wise Men came to the Christ Child, bearing gifts.

As some people do in other countries, you can observe Epiphany with what's called "Little Christmas"—you might have a bit of a feast, and exchange small gifties. At our house, John and I will make a special dinner to ring out the holidays.

There's another Epiphany celebration you might like, an old-time Irish tradition for the 12th day of Christmas: "Women's Christmas," or *Nollaig na mBan*. The men stay home, while females of all ages—toddlers to girls, mothers to elders—get together for feasting and dancing. While Women's Christmas was, for a long time, celebrated mostly in Ireland's rural areas, it seems to be coming back into popular Irish culture.

You could even start your own, wherever you are. Whether you're at a party or by yourself, if you're in the mood for dancing, I recommend the "Wassail Song"!

In any event, over the Twelve Days of Christmas, you can

embrace all those lovely holiday feelings of gratitude and love and abundance into the New Year. And beyond.

"I AM OUT WITH LANTERNS, looking for myself." —Emily Dickinson

Perhaps that ineffable feeling of awe, the transcendence you've hoped for is still within you. Waiting to be rediscovered. You can keep the holiday lights lit, keep your inner lantern shining, and have faith that you are already carrying the Christmas spirit in your heart, all year long.

A GOOD CHRISTMAS

"*M*yth is something that never was but always is."
—Thomas Mann

As I write this, it's the day of the Winter Solstice. An ethereal mist is drifting through the Foothills, giving an otherworldly aspect to the landscape. It puts me in a reflective mood, and I'm thinking over the last few weeks of this year's holiday season.

Every December 1st, when I bring out my Advent Calendars, I also pull out a worn manila folder I store with my Christmas decorations. In the folder, I keep a stack of holiday articles I've collected over the years.

In the weeks before Christmas, I always re-read three of the most thoughtful and transcendent pieces of my collection, which take on the Big Christmas Questions. Like eternal truth. Spiritual and religious beliefs. The power in the universe. Or why the holiday myths will always resonate.

Two are deeply meaningful essays, written in the late 1990s by a Congregationalist minister, titled, "Some look for the wrong kind of truth in the Christmas tale," and "Story assures the light will shine."

The minister, Anthony B. Robinson, closes that unforgettable essay with words I hold close:

"The Christmas story testifies to…the power of grace and new life, forever on the side of those brave enough to trust it."

THE THIRD ARTICLE is a yellowed newspaper clipping, also from the 90s, as faded as the others. It's one I cherish too, written by a columnist who explores the idea of a Hallmark card holiday: "Good Christmas better than the 'perfect' one."

But let's step back even further through the mists of time…

The writer of "Good Christmas" relates a very special Christmas Eve many decades ago, in 1968: the night the Apollo 8 spacecraft orbited the moon for the first time. Inside the craft, three astronauts, Frank Borman, James Lovell, and William Anderson were televised passing a bible back and forth between them, reading aloud.

Borman, Lovell and Anderson, perhaps the Three Wise Men of that moment in time, had chosen the Book of Genesis, sharing the verses about the Creation.

"…And God said let there be light. And God saw the light, and that it was good…"

It wasn't the Christmas story in the Book of Luke, or the Book of Matthew; yet it was a Christmas message all the same. The meaning, coming across loud and clear from so many thousands and thousands of miles away, was that we don't need perfect; all we need is *good*.

Bidding goodnight to the American people, that Christmas Eve of 1968, Mr. Borman said, "Merry Christmas, God bless all of you. All of you on the good Earth."

It's my wish for you and yours too. Be well, and may you

experience holidays that bring you comfort, quiet joys, and light.

THE CHRISTMAS VISITOR

An Irish Christmas "Novelette" from Susan's Village of Ballydara Fiction series

Susan Colleen Browne

To Meghann, my Irish girl

CHAPTER 1

The Christmas Visitor

"Granny, there's a light in the fairy cottage!"

Looking up from her sketchbook, Maeve O'Donoghue glanced at her granddaughter's animated face. "I can't imagine who'd be out in a snowstorm like this," she said mildly.

"Ava, you're seeing things again," her elder sister Nuala scoffed, but she dropped the DVD she was loading into the player and darted to the window. "As if anyone would want to step foot in that narky old mushroom house."

"I'm *not* seeing things," insisted Ava, pressing her face to the glass. "And it's *not* a mushroom house, it's a fairy house."

"Don't be an eejit," snapped Nuala. "There's no such thing as fairies—"

"Are too! That's why I made a fairy cairn—"

"And everyone says the place looks like a mushroom, with that ugly squished-in roof. Even Daddy—"

"Girls." Maeve sighed, and stretched her feet toward the peat fire her son Declan had built before he left for the pub. *Maybe it's a Christmas angel, out in the cottage,* she would've liked to tell Ava. What harm could there be, to encourage the little girl's imagination?

But given the child's tendency to get a bit overcome by her own flights of fancy, Maeve kept the words inside. The way things were going round here, with Francis gone, and Declan in a fair way to drowning his sorrows at Hurley's, the less said about Christmas the better. "It's likely only a trick of the snow, reflecting the light from our window," she said instead, hoping to diffuse yet another argument.

Even though it was the night before Christmas Eve, it was just another interminable evening spent alone with her granddaughters, the pair of them bored and inclined to squabble about anything—even what to call the shabby cottage next door where her in-laws had lived.

All through their marriage, Francis had told her, "You're a mystic, that's what you are," and teased her about living in her own little world. Still, she didn't know how much longer she could bear living in this one, the half-life she'd been forced into with him gone. Maeve felt like she was caught in some sort of time warp, where nothing ever changes. There'd always be the ache of loss in her breast, as if Francis had died only yesterday, instead of last summer. There'd never be an end to sitting here in the front room, doing sketches that she hadn't the heart to make into paintings, and trying to keep the girls' spirits up with their dad away every night. Never an end to trying to be a good granny when she'd hadn't done much mothering in the first place.

"Ava, would you get your nose off the window before you smudge the glass so bad we can't see out of it." Nuala jostled her little sister as she pulled the lace curtain wider. "Actually, Granny," she said, peering outside, "there *is* a light out there."

"See, I was right," Ava crowed, bouncing with excitement. "Let's go see who's there! It's probably a lost fairy and the snow tonight covered up the door to her underground house and now she's got to find a people's house to stay in *and* I want to see a fairy up close."

"And what're we meant to do with a *fairy?*" asked Nuala, a disdainful tilt to her freckled nose. "Invite her for tea?" At eleven, Nuala was normally more patient with her little sister, but these long nights must be getting to her too.

Maeve reluctantly set down her charcoal and crossed the room, feeling singularly unequipped to deal with a visitor. There it was all right, a tiny light in the old cottage a short distance away. It was probably a transient, who wouldn't want to be discovered and sent on his way. With Declan out, perhaps she'd better stay put—if she were to suss out the situation herself, she might be risking their safety.

But something in her was so desperate to break the monotony that she stepped to the closet and pulled out Francis' woolen overcoat. "I'm going to check the cottage. Whoever's out there might need a blanket, or a sandwich."

Nuala dropped the curtain. "Granny, you mustn't go! What if it's…somebody bad? Like the drug people in that selkie film we watched the other night?"

"Oooh, a *selkie*," breathed Ava. "Almost as good as a fairy."

"*Ondine*, you're talking about? I shouldn't think drug runners would bother with a remote little village in the West of Ireland," said Maeve, hiding a smile. She wiggled her feet into her ankle boots. "Unless they've come all the way to Ballydara to break into Murphy's shop and steal their Swiss chocolates."

"Then let's wait for Daddy to come home." Nuala wasn't one to take risks—a lot like Declan. "Or maybe we should ring the Garda."

"Please, let's go see who it is!" Ava ran to the closet to dig out her own coat. "I'll come too—"

"Ava, you can't go—"

"Yes I can—Granny, let me go!"

"Nuala, it'll be all right," Maeve soothed, assuming a confidence she didn't feel as she zipped up Ava's coat. The little one could use some distraction, and it wouldn't hurt for both girls to see a bit of charity in action. "If you like, you might stay by the phone," she said, helping Ava into her wellies. "If we're not back in five minutes, go ahead and ring up Hurley's for your dad."

Nuala ran to the kitchen, and before Maeve could turn the doorknob, she was back with not only the phone handset, but a torch. She handed it to Maeve, and stationed herself next to the window. "I'll be watching the clock, Granny."

"Thank you, love," said Maeve, and ushered Ava through the door. She plodded through the calf-deep snow, Ava marching beside her.

"D'you think it's a fairy? Can we bring her back to our house and give her some supper? Can we—"

"Darling, it's probably a lonesome fellow who needs a dry spot for the night. That's all." *Am I mad to face a stranger in the dark?* Maeve wondered, tuning out Ava's cannonade of questions. But if Francis was still alive, he would've gone out like a shot, keen to help. And after all, it was nearly Christmas.

So even if she'd done nothing about celebrating the holiday, she told herself as they trod the last few steps to the cottage, she ought to show some goodwill toward men.

Once at the door, Maeve made a show of stamping the snow off her boots before knocking, to avoid startling the man. But Ava had no such compunction. She yanked off a mitten and banged her little fist on the door, dislodging bits of peeling paint onto the snow. "Halloooo!"

Hearing a rustling, Maeve pulled out her torch, trying make herself look taller. The hinges creaked and the door opened. There, in a circle of light stood a woman. No, a girl really, just a slip of one, wrapped in a thick anorak. "Hallo yourselves," she said. An Irish girl. She pulled off her hood, and swept a cascade of curls away from her face.

Maeve dropped her torch. In the dim light, she made out the girl's delicate features and friendly smile. The stranger wasn't at all discomfited about trespassing, which caught Maeve off guard. "You're… all right?" was all she could come up with.

But her granddaughter was off and running. "I'm called Ava. What are you called? Where'd you come from? Can you come round to our house? I know how to make tea."

"Hallo, Ava—I'm called Hazel. Hazel Carey." The girl's smiled widened. "I'm from…well, just about everywhere."

Maeve found her voice. "Do you need anything? Have you enough to eat?"

"I'm grand," said Hazel. Maeve looked past her and saw that she'd set up a fairly comfy-looking camp. There was a small lantern on the floor emitting a blue-white light, a sleeping bag spread out, and next to it, an oversized rucksack. "I always travel with plenty to eat—"

"You look like a fairy girl," said Ava. "Are you a fairy? Are you lost? Please come round."

"No, I'm not lost—"

"Ava." Maeve remembered her five-minute limit just in time. "Run back to the house and tell Nuala we're fine."

"But Granny—"

"Now," Maeve said firmly, and picked up the torch she'd dropped. "We don't want your sister ringing the Garda, now do we? They'll…" she improvised quickly, "They'll take Hazel away."

"Oh!" Ava turned and flew back to the house, snow billowing around her feet.

Maeve faced the girl. "Do you—" She sensed a gentle soul in this Hazel, but what if her instincts were off? Just because this stranger was female, and a small one, didn't mean she couldn't be dangerous, despite her smile. Then she thought again of her husband, the way he'd always taken care of people, and the tightness in her chest began to recede. "This place is an awful kip, so cold, and no curtains to keep out the drafts," said Maeve. "And the mice—God save us, they're all over. Come back to the house and warm yourself."

"Oh, I'm used to camping out. And I don't mind mice a bit."

The girl was clearly made of sterner stuff than she looked. For some reason, whether concern, a need to break the tedium, or a wish to please Ava, Maeve found herself practically pleading with this girl. "We'd love to have you. Ava wouldn't be fit to live with if I couldn't persuade you to spend the evening with us."

Hazel gave her a direct look. "Are you sure? After all, I could be…anyone."

"That's probably what the innkeeper thought when he turned away Mary and Joseph," said Maeve, surprising herself. She'd never been the devout sort. Although it wasn't like her to be so insistent, she couldn't help saying, "And…it's Christmastime."

"Yes, it's Christmas," Hazel said, sounding pensive. She was silent for a moment, then, "I'd be delighted to come round. Who knows—there might not be room at the next inn." She bent and switched her lantern to a higher setting. "So I don't step on the mice when I return," she said, the smile back in her voice, and closed the door behind them.

As Hazel set off briskly, Maeve kept her torch in her pocket. "We hardly need a light tonight." She tried to sound casual, after pressuring the poor girl to visit. "It looks quite enchanting, doesn't it? The way the snow's illuminating everything." Down the road, the lights of the village glowed a translucent white-gold through the falling snow, and the colored lights strung around Hurley's pub created a blurry rainbow.

"Your granddaughters must be over the moon, to have a

white Christmas," said Hazel. "And to set your mind at ease, I'm actually not 'anyone.' I'm a friend of your son's."

"*Declan?*" Maeve nearly tumbled into the snow.

"That's how I turned up here," said Hazel. "He'd told me about his dad's place in Ballydara—that I couldn't miss the tumbledown cottage next door. And that if I ever came through County Galway, I should call round."

Still trying to grasp that the girl was acquainted with Declan, Maeve hadn't a clue what to say.

"I understand your husband passed away last summer," Hazel added, her voice turning sober, "but Declan said he was always a great one for visitors."

Maeve swallowed hard. "He...was."

"So I hoped...well, sure it's a bit of a cheek, but I guessed no one would mind if I camped out here. I found the key on a nail next to the door, just where Declan had said it would be." Then Hazel said, a little anxiously, "This is still his family home?"

"And mine," Maeve said, a little more at ease. So the girl wasn't as confident as she seemed. "I'm his mother. Maeve."

"If you don't mind my saying so," Hazel said, wading a bit more slowly, "you don't seem old enough to be his mam. Though I'm sure you've heard it before."

"I confess, I don't exactly get tired of it," said Maeve, disarmed, since Hazel hadn't said it to worm herself an invitation. "But then..." Something about this girl made her open up. "The years haven't been kind to my son. And lately, given the state of him, they won't get any kinder."

Hazel didn't ask why. As they tramped the last few steps to the house in silence, Maeve wondered if she'd hit bottom. That she'd become so lonely she was practically kidnapping strangers to bring into her home.

CHAPTER 2

Ava had the door already open. "I made Nuala put the kettle on for you, Hazel."

As Maeve removed her outdoor gear, Nuala stood behind Francis' old wingchair as if it was a shield, suspicion all over her face. "Hazel. That's a funny name. Like witchhazel." Resentment flared in her eyes. "Are you a witch?"

Nuala! Maeve almost scolded. But instead, she laid another sod on the fire and gave it a poke. "Hazel's no stranger." She tried to keep the reprimand from her voice. "She knows your dad."

Nuala ignored that. "Well, are you?"

"A witch?" Hazel wasn't at all nonplussed. "I'm more of the fairy persuasion," she said, smiling, as she slung her anorak onto the doorknob. "At least that's what my sister tells me."

Ava clapped her hands. "A fairy girl's in our house!"

"A good one or bad one?" Nuala challenged.

"Oooh, a good one," said Ava. "Bad fairies don't have pretty curls."

"How do you know my dad?" Nuala pressed, with the tenaciousness of a prosecuting solicitor. "He doesn't meet girls."

Hazel's smile widened. "Well, why would he? He has you. And Ava."

Nuala's uncharacteristic aggression seemed to collapse. "I...I guess he does."

"I met your dad last winter in America, when I was temping where he worked."

Ava, as if she did this every day, took Hazel's hand and looked up at her adoringly. "We lived in 'Merica too."

"Ah yes," said Hazel. "I was only at Ireland Place a short time, Nuala, but your dad actually talked about you quite a bit. He was so proud of your high marks at school. And he said you'd become quite a dab hand in the kitchen."

Nuala looked astonished. Maeve hid her amusement. Clearly, Hazel wouldn't be competition.

Ava tugged on Hazel's hand. "What about me? What'd he say about me?"

"He said that even though you weren't even five years of age, you'd such a personality you could make a gargoyle smile."

"What's a gargoyle?"

Hazel's eyes danced. "It's a statue that looks like the scariest creatures you can think of all mixed up, with the meanest face ever. So if you can make a gargoyle smile, it's like you're magic."

As Ava's face lit up, Maeve said, "That's our Ava, all right."

"There was a time though," Hazel went on, "that your dad mentioned you were awfully sick. With a bad tummy upset too."

"I 'frew-up," said Ava. "Lots."

"I'm sure you did. Your dad seemed terribly tired. I guessed he could hardly sleep for the worrying about you."

The kettle whistled. "Nuala, would you make the tea?" Maeve felt it was safe to ask. Then, to diffuse any remaining antipathy her elder granddaughter might harbor, she added, "Hazel can't stay long. And Ava, go help your sister, there's a love."

Ava said, "I'll make it 'specially good for you, Hazel," and the girls slipped into the kitchen.

"Sit here," said Maeve, pulling Francis' chair closer to the fire. She felt a pang as she caught his scent from the well-worn cushions. Hazel was gazing around the room—probably wondering why there weren't any holiday things out.

"Declan and I…we haven't gotten to any Christmas preparations," Maeve felt the need to explain. "With…Francis gone." Saying it, she felt so wobbly she took a deep breath to steady herself. "Six months to the day, actually."

"I can't imagine how hard the first Christmas must feel without him." Hazel sounded genuinely distressed. "I can still sense—" She broke off. "Well, the sadness here."

"Yes, there's been plenty of it," Maeve went on, intent on getting out all the bad news at once. "Especially for my son. His marriage broke up about the same time his dad died." She paused. "Actually, about the same day, if you can believe it."

"Poor man." Hazel watched the fire for a long moment. "I'd actually heard something about that too."

How? Maeve really wanted to know, but before she could work out a polite way to ask, Hazel went on, "How are the girls getting on without their mam? And their granddad?"

"That's the odd part," Maeve told her. After months of holding in her troubles, she couldn't help pouring them out in a flood. "Ava's always been headstrong, and she'd throw a tantrum as soon as look at you. But now she's overly eager to please. And Nuala was an easygoing child all her life, but as you see, she's become difficult and snappish. I try to let her express her feelings, not force her to keep them in like the girls of my generation were taught, but sometimes…"

"The bickering gets on your nerves a bit?"

"It does. Then there's Declan." Maeve rubbed at a charcoal smudge on her knuckle. *A trouble shared is a trouble halved* goes the old saying, but her heart felt even heavier in the telling. "I think losing his dad has been far harder for him than his marriage breaking up. Ever since Francis died, it's like he's trying to escape…"

Maeve trailed off. Whether her son was avoiding the reminders of his father here, or himself, Maeve didn't know. Not that it mattered. "He's away at the pub now every night."

"I wouldn't have guessed it," said Hazel. "He didn't seem the drinking sort."

"That's it—he's not. He told me he keeps it to one pint each night. But only last week, he said, 'if this goes on much longer,' and I guessed he was talking about not moving on, 'I could turn into a drinking man.' Declan has stayed busy with the girls, and some contract work these last months. But his heart's not in it. His heart's not in anything."

Hazel gave her a direct look. "When we worked together, he seemed quite keen on setting up some kind of enterprise back home. With his dad."

"With *Francis*?" This was the first Maeve had heard of it. "What sort of enterprise?"

"Well," said Hazel, "he seemed to be exploring his options, but he did mention he and his dad might try a hobby farm."

"Farming?" Astonished, Maeve reached for her charcoal to hide her reaction. "He spoke to you about *farming*?"

"That's what I do. I'm on the go a lot, taking jobs on small organic farms. I've actually worked up to being a farm apprentice."

"The travel sounds lovely." Maeve tried not to sound envious.

"It is, mostly," said Hazel. "When I was between farming gigs, Emma—that's my sister—got me set up temping at Ireland Place, where she was a co-worker of Declan's. Now and then, he and I would chat about the farms I worked on. He said he wouldn't expect to make money from a small hobby farm, but it would be great crack for his kids."

"He's…never mentioned it," Maeve said slowly. "Farming, I mean."

The memory came to her, from Declan's early childhood. When Francis had kept a few chickens and goats. Declan had come up with a name for each one, and he and his dad would spend hours tending to them. They'd even fixed up her in-laws' decrepit byre for a coop. But when Francis' teaching duties expanded, she'd been unwilling to cut back on her painting to help look after the animals. So he'd given them away, to a family in the next townland. How was it she'd never thought Declan would mourn over it?

"I'm no expert, of course," Hazel was saying, "but in the last two years, I've worked at three different farms—in New Zealand, one near Seattle, and my present job is in upstate New York."

"New York, is it?"

Hazel smiled at her. "It's a grand life, farming, being your own boss. Declan could give a wee farm a go, see where it leads."

Maeve looked more closely at the girl. Had her son been attracted to her, back in America? Sure, he wouldn't be the first to fancy a pretty girl far too young for him, especially since his wife had spent the better part of their marriage away for work. But Hazel's eyes were steady, her face open—no undercurrents there.

"He's not the sort to turn his life upside down, all for a dream," Maeve said finally. God knows Declan's wife Sue was champion of that department. "Especially with two girls to raise."

"I rather thought so," said Hazel.

Her son's problems suddenly felt overwhelming. Maeve changed the subject. "You must've come home, then, for Christmas?"

Hazel looked rueful. "I never like leaving my farms, but I promised Emma I'd make a holiday visit. She's in Dublin now."

"Here in Galway, you're some distance from there," observed Maeve, hoping to draw her out more.

"I am, yeah. I came up to the West to…well, for a taste of the country." Hazel's gaze went to the fire again, and Maeve wondered if getting a "taste of the country" was a way to avoid her family? "And I thought, if I run into Declan, why not say Happy Christmas to him while I'm in the area?"

The girls clattered back in, Nuala balancing a tray. It held a teapot, three mugs and a teacup, set on one of the good tea towels. "We made hot chocolate for you, Hazel," said Ava, wearing a milk-chocolate moustache on her upper lip. "Chocolate's my very favorite thing."

"I can tell." Hazel ruffled Ava's dark hair, with the shaggy fringe cut by Nuala's inexpert hands. "I love chocolate myself."

Maeve watched, bemused, as her elder granddaughter played hostess, passing a steaming mug to Hazel, then she poured a cup of tea for her granny. "These are scones I baked," Nuala said shyly, proffering a plateful. "Daddy said his appetite was a bit off this week, else they'd be gone by now. In case they were a bit stale, I heated them up."

"Lovely," said Hazel. She took two, buttered them abundantly, and tucked in. The girl certainly ate like a farmer, and Maeve smiled to herself. Hazel said between bites, "So then, girls, what do you hope Father Christmas will bring you?"

CHAPTER 3

Nuala sobered. "I don't think that Dad—"

"I want him to bring me a fairy doll!" Ava took a noisy slurp from her mug. "A big one, with curly goldy-brown hair. Like yours."

"So, you like dollies, then?"

"I like fairies better," said Ava. She set down her mug, then crawled beneath the chair Hazel sat in. Pulling out a shoebox, she showed Hazel its contents—her collection of finger-sized fairy dolls. "Look how many! Will you play fairies with me?"

"I would *love* to play fairies," Hazel said, as if she'd been waiting all her life to do it. *I should try for a bit of that enthusiasm myself*, Maeve thought. "But first, let's hear what Nuala would like from Father Christmas."

Nuala only shrugged. She'd probably guessed that Declan hadn't bought any Christmas gifts, Maeve thought with a pang.

Hazel took another big bite of the scone. "Come on then, surely there's something you want."

"Well…" Nuala looked guarded, then she burst out, "I want… animals."

"Ah," said Hazel. "A pet? Like a cat, or a puppy?"

"I'd like a pet fairy," Ava said dreamily, playing dollies at Hazel's feet.

"No, like a…" Nuala lowered her voice. "My auntie has horses, so a horse would be great. Or maybe a lamb? Or just some chickens. But of course we can't have them."

Holy Mother of God. Maeve could've fallen out of her chair. The child had never even hinted at such things.

"Why not?" asked Hazel.

Nuala twisted her fingers together. "I know having animals is awfully dear. Like thousands and thousands of euro."

Hazel nodded thoughtfully. "Sometimes."

"Back in America, I heard Daddy have a row with my mam about money." Her mouth seemed to tremble. "Mam's last film project took every penny they had, he said. I know we still haven't any extra."

Declan hadn't told her. Maeve felt shame, for letting her grief—or perhaps just as much, the disorientation of widowhood—blind her to the grandchildren's needs. How dreadful for young Nuala, to have heard such hurtful words, and be worried about money still, only the girl hadn't felt comfortable coming to her granny for reassurance.

Worse, here it was Christmas, and she hadn't bestirred herself to even hang a sprig of greenery, or come up with any gifts for her granddaughters. She could hardly look at Hazel—the girl must be thinking, *what kind of a granny are you anyway?*

But Hazel only leaned closer to Nuala. "Here's the thing, though. You've no need for buckets of euro to enjoy horses or sheep or chickens."

"Or fairies," put in Ava, marching her dolls across the rug.

"But when I hear my dad say we can't afford this or that," said Nuala, her face bleak, "I'm sure that includes animals."

"Well, then, here's what you do," Hazel said cheerfully. "When you next see your auntie, you ask her to show you how to take care of—"

"But Auntie lives far, far away!" said Ava.

"All my aunties live in Dublin, said Nuala, a little mournfully. "We don't get to visit very often."

"Well, then," said Hazel, "there's…plenty of farm families near here, right?"

"Well, yes," admitted Nuala. "Granddad was friends with a farmer, Mr. Whelan."

Maeve thought a shadow crossed the young woman's face. "You could…you could ask your dad to go round with you to Mr. Whelan," said Hazel. "Or another farmer, and you tell them you'd like to help out. That you'll work really hard—mucking out barns, feeding animals, whatever they need. And that you don't want pay, you'll do it for the experience."

"Is that how you learned about farming?" asked Nuala.

"That's right, even though I'm from Dublin."

"But…would any farmer want me? I'm only eleven."

"Sure they would. Most farmers need all the help they can get. And farm kids are doing chores and driving tractors before they've started primary school. Any farmer'd love to have you—all you've got to do is introduce yourself."

"Oh." Nuala looked hopeful. "Maybe…I could do that."

"Ah, sure you can. It'll be the next best thing to having your own animals. Then, when you're older, you can get proper job and save your money, and have your own place."

"There's just one thing." Nuala bit her lip. "I'll need muck boots. I'd a pair of wellies when I was littler, but my feet are miles too big for them now."

"You can always borrow some, right? Might you know any neighbor ladies in the village, the smiley kind, who do lots of gardening?"

"Well…" Nuala crumbled some bits of scone in her fingers. "Mrs. Moore, she always chats with us while she tends her roses. And we know Miss Bridie O'Donnell—she keeps a garden too."

"Well then, all you have to do is call round to say hi, and bring the ladies some of your lovely scones. One or the other is sure to have an extra pair of wellies just lying about, waiting for a new owner. You just have to ask."

Nuala suddenly looked lit up from the inside. "Okay." She finished off her scone in one enormous bite.

Hazel clapped her hands on her knees. "Right, Maeve, now it's your turn. We haven't heard what you'd like for Christmas."

Ignoring the surprise on both girls' faces, that a grown-up should ask for a gift, Maeve felt a twist in her stomach. What did she want? For widowhood to be…easier? For Declan to be happy again? Or perhaps selfishly, to be able to paint again? She grasped her charcoal with trembling fingers, and drew her sketchbook to her chest, hugging it like a security blanket. "Oh, all I want is a happy Christmas."

"Might I ask," said Hazel, "what's that you're working on?"

The girl must've picked up some of that openness from Americans. Maeve wasn't used to folk inquiring about her art. God knows it had created plenty of conflict in the past. But she reluctantly passed the sketchbook over. "Can you guess?"

Hazel studied the rough portrait for a long moment, then met Maeve's eyes. Maeve saw sympathy there. "Declan." She'd seen then, the deeper crease between son's brows. The bleakness in his eyes.

"Granny used to be an artist," volunteered Nuala.

Maeve winced. "It's a hobby," she said with false brightness. She pictured the stacks of canvases stored in the closet upstairs —her cherished life's work, now shoved alongside the other household clutter. She thought of the studio Francis had planned to build for her after he retired—a proper detached studio, roomy and full of light, not like the spare bedroom she'd used for years. Now the studio sketches they'd made together were buried behind the paintings, gathering dust. "A bit of noodling, to help while away the long winter evenings."

Hazel passed back the sketchbook. "It's gorgeous." She gave Maeve a significant look. "But back to what you'd like Father Christmas to bring you, it's like I told Nuala here. Asking is all it takes, really, to get what you want. You just ask."

"Em...Hazel?" Nuala bounced out of her chair to collect the mugs, piling them onto the tray helter-skelter. "Might you... maybe...help us put up some Christmas decorations?"

"Oh, yes!" Ava squealed. "Let's decorate for Christmas! I'll play fairies later." She grabbed Hazel's hand in a take-no-prisoners grip, and practically yanked their guest out of her chair.

"First, we'd better ask your granny if it's all right." Hazel gave Maeve a questioning look. "I wouldn't want to presume."

"That would be lovely." Smiling at all three girls, Maeve waved them off, and they tripped up the stairs. Once they were out of sight, she sagged back into her chair. She should feel guiltier, letting a stranger take on what she should be doing, but she was too grateful for the girl's energy. The energy she and Declan had lacked all these months.

The three soon trotted back down to the front room, Hazel carrying Francis' oversized box of Christmas things. He'd always loved to decorate the house, and as the younger girls pulled out the Father Christmas figures, the giant nutcracker, and the Nativity pieces, Maeve's throat went tight. Still, as Hazel ooh'd and ah'd over each item, she managed to join in. Then, while Hazel untangled strings of lights, Nuala and Ava set the bric-a-brac on every flat surface in the room.

Their holiday spirit was contagious. "I've an idea," Maeve said, rising from her chair. "Let's put out a big glass bowl—we can fill it with the tree ornaments." *Since we've no tree.*

When she returned from the kitchen, Ava reverently placed each bauble in the bowl. As a final touch, Nuala helped Hazel drape fairy lights on the curtain rod at the front window. "Lookit, lookit!" Ava pranced round the room. "It's the prettiest Christmas ever!"

Their visitor pressed the plug into the socket, then stood back to admire. "What do you think?"

"Everything's beautiful." Nuala's eyes shone. "Now it feels like Christmas."

Hazel straightened the lace curtain. "We're missing one thing, though, aren't we? For a proper Christmas Eve, you'll need a candle in the window." She grinned at Maeve. "I haven't been away from Ireland so long that I've forgotten *that*."

Nuala's face fell. "We haven't any candles. I looked yesterday."

"You never know," Hazel said, with what Maeve had already come to see as her boundless optimism. "Maybe something will turn up."

And maybe we'll wake up to find a fairy ring in the middle of the front room, Maeve thought, then she noticed a weary look on Hazel's face. Oh dear—the girl had been traveling all over creation, and here she'd let their guest take on the kids for the entire evening. "Girls, Hazel's been traveling—she's probably jet-lagged. She'll need to go to bed soon."

"What's that, jet-lag?" Ava asked.

"Really tired." Hazel rubbed her temple. "I confess, I'm feeling quite knackered all of a sudden. Time to say goodnight then." She pulled her anorak off the doorknob.

"Can't you stay longer, Hazel?" Ava tugged at Hazel's fleece shirt. "Please?"

"You could sleep on our couch," said Nuala. "Couldn't she, Granny? I'd make her a proper breakfast and everything."

"We'd love to have you," Maeve said. "No need to sleep in the cold."

Hazel hesitated. She crouched next to Ava, took her little hand, and to Maeve's astonishment, kissed it. Then she let go, standing up to shrug into her anorak. "Thank-you—that's so kind. But I've got used to New York winters—my sleeping bag will keep me warm. Anyway, I've an early…ride to Dublin in the morning." She reached for the doorknob. "It was great meeting you all."

"Good-bye, then," said Nuala, her eyes pink. She picked up the sugar bowl and teapot, heading for the kitchen. "Happy Christmas, Hazel," she said over her shoulder.

"We're...so grateful you came round," Maeve said. She'd never have thought it would be so hard to part with someone she'd known for less than a few hours. "Have a safe journey."

Ava's pleading look turned stormy, and Maeve thought, *God, we're in for it now. I should've known all this unnaturally good behavior wouldn't last.* But to her surprise, in this night of many surprises, the child suddenly grinned at Hazel and hugged her. "Will you come back, Hazel?"

"I'd like that very much. If I'm invited."

Maeve's smile widened. "We'd love nothing better."

Ava briefly pressed her face to Hazel's stomach, then gazed up at her and whispered, "Will you bring your baby?"

Hazel looked at Maeve with an arrested expression. "Oh, that's not poss—"

"Our Ava's got an imagination, that one," broke in Maeve, embarrassed. She glanced at her granddaughter. "Ava, Hazel hasn't a baby."

"Actually..." Hazel paused for a long moment. "I...don't know." She stared into the middle distance, an unreadable expression on her face. Then she looked down at Ava, smoothing her hair. "You're a wise one, aren't you?" Maeve saw her hand tremble. She added very quietly, "You never know, do you? It could be the Annunciation, come to life."

"What's that, 'nunciation?" Ava tightened her grip on Hazel.

Hazel went silent again. She finally said, "It's part of the Christmas story, when the Angel came to Mary, to tell her she had Baby Jesus in her tummy."

And in the Gospel the young Mary visited the older woman Elizabeth, thought Maeve, thunderstruck. *And changed her life.*

"Do you have Baby Jesus in your tummy?" Ava asked.

Was that a shadow in Hazel's eyes? Then she smiled. "No, pet," she murmured. "Baby Jesus was born a long, long time ago." She dropped a kiss on Ava's head and gently disentangled herself. "Right then. Off I go."

As Hazel opened the door, Nuala emerged from the kitchen, looking as if she wanted a hug too. Instead, she crossed her thin arms. She was Declan's daughter, after all, Maeve thought. Not one for taking chances. "See you," she only said. Swiping her nose, she headed for the stairs.

As Hazel closed the door behind her, Ava raced to the window and pulled aside the lace curtain. Maeve joined her, to watch Hazel wade through the swirling snow toward the old cottage. She curved her arm around Ava's little shoulders. "Wasn't it a lovely evening?"

Ava leaned her head against Maeve's hip. "Do you think Hazel's a fairy?"

An automatic "no" rose to Maeve's lips, then she thought, *ah, the world will stifle a child's spirit soon enough.* "Sometimes real-life people are so special, they're like angels or good fairies, bringing lovely and magical things to everyone they meet. Like Hazel. But I think you're *our* Christmas angel, Ava."

"I'd rather be a fairy," said Ava, "but I like angels too."

CHAPTER 4

After tucking the children into bed, Maeve had just settled into Francis' chair when she heard a soft scratch on the door. It had to be Hazel. Had she changed her mind about staying? In a flash, Maeve had the door open.

Hazel was on the stoop, an odd-shaped parcel in one arm. "Here I am, the proverbial bad penny, but I remembered something."

"Oh...Hazel." Maeve wanted to draw her back inside, but saying goodbye twice would be too hard.

With her free hand, Hazel pulled something from her anorak pocket. A golden votive candle. "For your window—it's made of beeswax, from the farm. I always have a few in my backpack, in case I can't get my lantern recharged."

"Lovely." Something to remember Hazel by. As if they'd need reminding. "Thank you."

"And something else," Hazel said, and handed over the parcel —a lumpy plastic sack. "A bit of Christmas cheer for the girls. Might you have some pretty holiday paper to wrap things up in?"

Maeve opened the sack, and a grapefruit-sized lump rose in

her throat. Pulling out a pair of brand-new hand-tooled cowboy boots, she choked out, "For Nuala?"

"Emma, God love her, is forever spending her money on gifts for me. Lovely things, all of them, that I've no use for. In this case, it's clear she's rather clueless about farm life, don't you think?"

Maeve managed, "Dear, we can't possibly accept—"

"I was going to give the boots away anyway, to Mam's parish or something. But so much nicer to give to a friend, don't you think? And here's something for Ava too."

With Maeve's hands full, Hazel took the sack from her and drew out a book. "Another gift from Emma, that I was going to give away."

It was a picture book. *The Wee Christmas Cabin of Carn-na-ween*. And a limited edition, by the look of it. Tears rose to Maeve's eyes. "I don't know what to say—it's absolutely brilliant."

"It'll be easier to wrap than the boots, I'm thinking." Hazel put the storybook back in the sack, and pressed the parcel into Maeve's hands.

"The girls will be dazzled—but really Hazel, I shouldn't want to take anything from you, after all you did for us—"

"It'd be a favor." Hazel looked away. "I'm not keen on a lot of baggage, you see. Or carting around all sorts of stuff when I'm off to the next job."

"But I haven't a present for you…"

"Oh, my rucksack's full anyway, and with the extra luggage fees these days…" Hazel's gaze returned to hers. "Besides, I might need to…lighten my load a bit."

As you lightened mine… Maeve gathered her courage. "It's a complete mystery to me, how Ava could have come up with such a thing—I mean, a *baby*."

"Oh, some things just can't be explained," Hazel said slowly.

"I'm a bit gobstruck myself, that I didn't…" she trailed away, looking a little…lost.

There was so much Maeve wanted to ask her, but had no right to. *How are you feeling? Might you take a test?* She was nearly overcome by a feeling of protectiveness. *And how will you get on, if you've a baby on the way and you're on your own?*

Maeve was struck by a new kind of grief. So then, this connection is what she'd missed out on, not having a daughter. She'd been the one to insist on limiting their family to one child, even though Francis had been keen for a houseful.

But you've two granddaughters, Maeve reminded herself. Girls to cherish, girls who can grow up to be the best friends you ever have. That is, if you learn to look around you, to appreciate the gift you've been given… She realized she did have something to give to Hazel.

Setting down the boots and sack, Maeve reached for her sketchbook. She tore off the paper she'd been working on. "For you."

Hazel took a long, thoughtful look at the rough portrait of Declan, then briskly rolled it up, and tucked it inside her anorak. "I'll look after it, I promise."

"Look after *yourself*, all right?" Maeve said. *And your baby, if there is one.*

"I will." Hazel touched her middle, as if she'd read Maeve's mind.

Then Maeve was struck by something, so strongly her knees wobbled. "Did you come here to see Declan, love? I just remembered—he'd traveled to New York City last month, but he never mentioned going up to—"

"*Declan?*" Hazel actually giggled. "You mean, is he…um, I promise you, he's only a mate."

Maeve flushed with embarrassment. "I had to ask." Despite her relief, her heart was heavy. There'd be no earthly reason for Hazel to be in their lives in the future.

"I know," Hazel said. "He's a lovely man, but it's not me he's sweet on." Before Maeve could take that in, Hazel said, "Well, then, off again. Say hi to Declan for me, will you?" She hesitated, then with a quick "God bless," she kissed Maeve's cheek, and was gone.

Maeve stood in the open doorway, her hand pressed to her cheek. *Blessed art thou among women,* Elizabeth had said to her young visitor Mary. *Hazel, you've blessed us more than you'll ever know.* She watched the girl disappear into the old cottage for the second time, finally realizing what she really wanted for Christmas. For her family to come back to life. And after Hazel's visit tonight, they were halfway there.

When the cold air finally brought her back to herself, she closed the door, and stuffed the gorgeous boots back inside the plastic sack. Curious…the sack was from the Irish Arts Centre in New York City, of all places.

Promising herself to wrap the gifts before she went to bed, Maeve set the sack on the ottoman next to her chair, then went to the kitchen for a saucer and some matches. Returning to the front window, she swept the lace curtain up over the curtain rod, which gave a misty look to the white lights. Maeve set the small golden candle on the saucer and lit it. To help Declan find his way home.

And perhaps, before too long, he'd find his *way.*

She set another chunk of peat on the fire, and settled back into the armchair. Wrapping herself in a throw blanket, Maeve gave in to the waves of sleepiness washing over her. *Maybe I'll find my way too.*

CHAPTER 5

Maeve roused to a muffled banging, and opened her eyes as the front door snapped shut. "Declan," she said, blinking her eyes against the lamplight, and laughed a little at the sight of her tall son, covered in snow. "Oh, the state of you! You look like the Abominable Snowman."

"Mam, you're all right then? You and the girls?"

Maeve took in the strange, wild-eyed look on Declan, his face unnaturally red. Her heart sank. Had he finally taken to the drink then? And on Christmas Eve? "You're not…jarred, are you?"

"No! No, Mam, I swear I'm not." He whacked snow off his coat, and it flew all over the entryway like a small blizzard. "I swear to God, Mam, I'm stone sober, but tell me, before I decide I've gone completely round the bend, did you notice a light in the old cottage tonight?"

"Yes!" Maeve sat up straight. "That would be our visitor, who's staying the night. Haz—"

"But there's no one there. I've just gone round and banged on the door—"

"Don't tell me you've woken the poor girl!"

"What poor girl?"

"Your friend Hazel is staying there, just come from America."

Declan looked floored. "Not Hazel Carey? Little thing, curly hair? She was here tonight?"

"Yes—we had the loveliest evening with her, then she went back to the cottage for the night." Maeve pushed herself out of the chair, tossed the throw around her shoulders, and stumbled to the door. "I need to see if she's all right," she said, jamming her feet into the boots she'd left out. "I asked her to stay here inside, in the warm, but she insisted on sleeping out in that old kip." She flung the door open and stepped into the snow.

"Trust me, Mam, the place is empty," Declan said, right behind her. Maeve tromped to the cottage, and as they approached the door, she said, "Look, there are no tracks—of course she's still in there."

"Mam, it's been snowing like hell," Declan said. "Enough to cover anything." Still, he called, "Hazel? It's me, Declan." He rattled the knob, but it was locked, as usual. He checked the nail on the wall for the key. It was gone. "Hazel? Are you in there?" Bare-handed, he knocked on the door until Maeve thought his knuckles would bleed, but there was no reply.

Maeve lurched to the nearest window and peered inside. Searching for a dark shape on the floor, where she'd seen Hazel's sleeping bag earlier, she hoped against hope the girl was simply so tired she could sleep through all sorts of caterwauling. But the interior was bare—not a rucksack, a sleeping bag, or a sleeping girl to be seen.

"Mam, she's gone. And you must be freezing. Let's go back to the house."

"Why would she leave in the middle of the night?" Maeve asked despairingly. Then she remembered the shadow on Hazel's face. *I'm not keen on baggage*, she'd said. Was Hazel avoiding something? Or someone?

I'll never know.

Declan stood back from the old place, his hands in his pockets, head bent. Then he looked up at her. "We both aren't a bit mad? Did the pair of us only imagine the light? And you dreamed up Hazel?"

"Anything's possible," Maeve said, forlorn. "But the girls will tell you all about her. You should've seen their faces tonight—the fancy they had for her."

Declan took her arm, and steered her toward the house. "I'm relieved she came here, even if she's gone and left us. Because I was convinced it was Dad, haunting the place."

"Your dad? For the love of God—"

"Let's get inside, and I'll tell you the lot."

CHAPTER 6

Feeling suddenly shaky, Maeve was glad for her son's supporting arm as they tramped back to the house. Once inside, Declan shrugged off his coat, while Maeve shook the snow from her throw blanket. "I'll put the kettle on."

"The tea can wait, Mam—I've got to tell you what happened tonight." Declan collapsed onto the couch. "Why I'm thinking I'd gone crackers…" He swiped at his hair, the melting snow from it dripping on his face. "I was sitting alone at the bar tonight, like I've been doing all these months. People have been respectful—they generally leave me to my brooding. I know they pity me because of Sue leaving—but they don't know it's Dad I'm missing."

Maeve nodded. She'd heard the whispers.

"Earlier, everyone was talking about the snowstorm. Only the old ones have seen snow like this. But Pat Hurley said to me, 'Your dad was a great one for snow. Years ago, when you were very small, it was coming down almost like this. He went out and collected all the kids in the village, even us big lads too, and organized a snowball fight. Your dad, he lobbed a good one at me, but I ducked. It hit Father Monaghan right in the kisser.'"

Maeve smiled, remembering the old ones in the village were scandalized. The schoolmaster smacking the good Father!

"Then it strikes me, like a snowball in the face, that's it's been exactly six months since Dad died. And here we've got to face our first Christmas without him, and I just can't bear it. I think, what the hell, I can't feel any worse, so I say to Pat, 'I'll take another round.'" He looked grim.

Maeve said, "Really, Declan, it's hardly a crime—"

"But I'd broken my promise to myself. Anyway, Pat takes his time with the pint, puts a nice head on the glass, while I'm thinking, will you hurry it up, man? I'm ready to get really jarred tonight. Pat sets the pint down in front of me and turns away. I down about half of it in one gulp, then all of a sudden, I hear, *What are you about?*

"'Did you just say something?' I ask Pat. 'Not me,' he says, over his shoulder, then goes about his business. Then I hear it again. *What are you about, lad?*

"I take a furtive look round the pub, thinking maybe there's a wise guy in the place, someone who knows a few ventriloquist tricks. But no one's paying me any attention. And the voice is still there—it sounds just like Dad, giving me a proper scold. *After all you've been through, why turn to the drink now?*

"I start thinking, surely a couple of pints hasn't made me delusional? But I've a few things to say back to whoever's talking to me. So I leave the bar, too rattled to remember that I haven't paid Pat, and practically run outside. Only there's a few fellows out there getting a smoke, and I can hardly start talking to someone who's not there, or folk will think I'm not just an anti-social tosser, but completely daft.

"And now that I'm out of the din of the pub, I realize the voice doesn't only sound like Dad, it *is* Dad. He's not a ghost—there's no sign of him. But the voice in my ear is the one I've heard all my life—although right now, he's giving me a real bollocking, like he never did when he was alive. I want to tell him my side, but I need to find some privacy. So I head for St. MacDara's. On the way, I look down the road toward our place, and I see a light on in the old cottage. Of course, I'm imagining it, just like this bit with Dad talking to me. Since I'm clearly mad, I'll just see what else he has to say."

"Declan, you're not—"

"Mam, just let me tell it. So I ignore the light, and soon I'm sitting on the church steps, right in the snow, like the nutter I am. It's where we last talked, Dad and I, the night of his retirement party, when I told him about Sue leaving, and I knew his heart was breaking for me. But it's not breaking now. He's right fierce, asking me, *what am I doing at the pub, with two sweet girls waiting for me at home?* I don't know what to say, because it's true, but after a fair bit of this I just want him to shut up. So I say, 'A man's not allowed to grieve for his dad?'

Ah sure, lad, but half a year's gone by. Why are you still moping about?

"'Christ above, Dad, you died,' I tell him. 'I'll bloody well grieve for you if I want to!'

Grief's one thing, but don't use it to let your life turn to shambles.

"Well, he's got me there. But thank Jesus, he's stopped talking. By now, I'm feeling really disoriented and half frozen too. To get my bearings, I look toward our place again, and the light's still on in the cottage. So I'm still imagining it.

And now that Dad has finally shut up, I start thinking about how I loved the old place when I was a kid, and all the times I'd be playing outside with my mates, after Granddad died. On the way home, I'd pop in to Granny's for tea and a treat, and Dad was almost always there, keeping her company.

So there on the church steps, I'm even imagining stopping by the cottage tonight, sure I'll find Granny at the hob, and Dad eating his third slice of soda bread. Then he breaks up my little dream—he hasn't finished after all. *Pull yourself together, son,* he says, *and go away home.*

"I can't argue with that, especially since my arse has just about turned to ice. So I scramble to my feet and glance at the cottage, and as I'm watching, the light goes out. Now, I'm thinking I might've imagined the light being on, but I'm sure I didn't imagine seeing it go off. And now that I'm back to reality, of course I know Granny's long dead, and now Dad is too. So who's in the cottage?

"I start running. There could be an intruder at our place, so I've got to get home, make sure you and the girls are all right. But just as I pass Murphy's shop, Dad starts in again. *Aren't you forgetting something?* he says. *You haven't a Christmas tree.* I stop sharpish, and see the shop still has a few Christmas trees in the lot round the back. 'The shop's closed,' I tell him, 'And I've got to check on Mam and the kids.' All the same, he insists. *A proper father would bring home a tree for his girls.*

"The only trees left are a pair of small, scraggly ones, and one giant article that must be over three meters high. Of course I can't bring home the undersized twigs, so I figure, go for it. I nip over the fence, then haul the giant tree back over it, all the while praying the Garda hasn't driven over from Knockferry, to catch me nicking the biggest fecking Christmas tree in Ireland.

"But lucky for me, they're not in Ballydara tonight. Good job it is too, since I'd be easy to catch, dragging the tree home in the snow. Then Dad says, *Fair play to you, son—it's a grand tree, so it is.* I swear I hear him chuckling. *And look, the snow's coming down so hard it'll cover up the evidence of your crime.*

"Then as I draw closer to the cottage, I suddenly feel my head clear, and dead silence. I know he's gone." Declan heaved a great sigh. "Then it's just as I told you. I banged on the cottage door, then I came in here."

Maeve wasn't about to write off his encounter with his father—things like that happened more often than folk thought. Like Hazel had said, *Some things just can't be explained.* "You do realize, love, you're as sane as anyone else."

"I'm aware that your brain can conjure up things, trick your senses, if that's what you mean." Declan stared at his clasped hands. "Like if you've been riding the train all day, and after you've gotten off and gone to bed, you can still feel the rocking motion. But still—"

"Could be, your dad's a bit restless, there in the afterlife." Maeve tilted her head, trying to catch his eye. "You know how proud he was of you, how much he wanted to keep you safe."

"He was, at that." Declan's mouth tightened, as if he was trying not to weep. "The best friend I ever had."

"And maybe he couldn't rest until he'd helped you put yourself to rights."

"Dad always said you were the mystical one of the family, but maybe…oh, hell, maybe I don't need to know the hows or whys. In a way, it was grand to hear his voice again." Declan rubbed at the remaining moisture on his face, then looked around the room. "The decorations!" His mouth curved a bit, then a proper grin broke out on his face. "Jaysus, maybe Dad visited here too, to get the house ready for Christmas."

"Silly boy," Maeve said fondly. "The girls and Hazel did it. And Hazel gave us the candle, to put in the window."

"She's a great kid," Declan said, with no trace of a lover's tone. "She never stays long in one place, though."

So then, it was as Hazel said. Her son had no unrequited passion for a girl young enough to be his daughter, and pregnant to boot. Ready to tell Declan about the baby, Maeve stopped herself in time. He'd find out, if he was meant to.

"I'd like to text Hazel, tell her I'm sorry I missed her," he added. "But she has no use whatsoever for mobiles. She's rather a throwback, she always said."

"I sensed that myself," said Maeve.

"I only hope she remembers to send us the cottage key—it's the only one we have." Declan pushed himself off the couch and blew out the little candle. "Better save a bit of her candle for tomorrow, don't you think?" Then, gazing out the window, he said, "Did she say she was spending Christmas in Dublin? With her... family?"

"A short visit," Maeve said cautiously. "Then she's back to the States."

Silence. Then, "She didn't mention...her sister, did she?"

So it was the sister then. Maeve smiled to herself. A good sign, that her son had some life in him after all. "Emma, I think she's called. I gathered Hazel's quite fond of her."

When Declan didn't answer, Maeve peeked at his profile. He had a faraway look on his face. "Right," he said finally, then he turned to face her. "It must be close to two am," he said. "Before we're asleep on our feet, I'd better bring in the tree."

After he wrestled the monster fir indoors, Maeve admitted, "I've no idea where your dad kept the Christmas tree stand." She fetched a bucket, and after they'd seated the tree, she held it upright while Declan went out to the front garden. After no small amount of snow-clearing, he retrieved some stones from Ava's fairy cairn, and brought them inside to secure the tree.

"We've got until the snow melts, to come up with an explanation for how her cairn got caved in," Maeve said, feeling more lighthearted than she had since Francis died.

"We're a mad pair, aren't we?" Declan said, brushing snow off his hair.

"That we are," Maeve agreed, and curled back up in her chair. She was as wet as Declan, from tussling with the snow-laden tree. "Part of me would like to decorate this beast and surprise the kids—"

"But of course, they'd love to do it," Declan finished. Then he did something unexpected. Crouching next to her chair, he took her hand. "Mam, you've been great—giving up so much for us to stay here."

She didn't know what to say, only squeezed his in return. These last months, she'd found comfort in holding his hand, appreciating the sturdiness of it, a man's hand, not the little boy's she'd once held. Only not enough.

"Sure, Dad wouldn't have blinked at the inconvenience, but you—I know the sacrifices you've made. For starters, letting go of your workspace so the girls could have a bedroom."

"Really, I didn't mind," Maeve said, for once not feeling it was a lie.

"But you've neglected your work altogether so you could look after them all these months, while I've been in this...I don't know, *fog*. Not knowing what to do with myself. But Mam..." Declan's gaze was intent. "This mad thing with Dad talking to me—well, it's convinced me that things have to change round here. For one thing, it's time you got your life back."

"Maybe...I could start painting again," said Maeve.

"Good. Because I'm done spending my evenings at the pub—time for me to be a proper father again too. Like Dad told me."

"You always have been," Maeve said softly. "You just needed a bit of reminding."

He grinned crookedly, then rose to his feet. "So then, we've got a Christmas tree, but no presents. When I go to Murphy's tomorrow to pay for the tree, I'll find a few trinkets for the girls—"

"Mother of God!" Maeve jackknifed out of her chair. "I almost forgot—" She reached for the parcel, and pulled out its contents. "Look what Hazel brought!"

"Good Lord!" Declan examined the storybook first. "'Wee Christmas Cabin'...this story seems familiar. I think Dad might've read it to me. How's that for coincidence?" Then he ran an admiring hand over the boots. "I won't find anything to beat these in Murphy's shop," he said ruefully. "Hazel's something, isn't she?"

"Ava thought she was a fairy," said Maeve, feeling teary again.

"Maybe she is." Declan gave her shoulders a squeeze. "The book just now reminded me—the way Dad was so keen on all the fairy legends. He told me that when there's a white Christmas, the fairies leave their special houses and go out and about in the snow, to see the wonder of it."

Well, Francis, said Maeve silently, *you might be onto something.* "Fairy or not, I just hope Hazel's boots fit Nuala, the way our girl is growing."

"Yeah…see how well they're made?" Declan slid his hand into one boot. "Wait—there's something in here." He drew out a folded-up sheet of glossy paper, and set the boot down.

"A label?" Maeve asked.

"No…seems to be a brochure." He passed it to her.

She unfolded the sheet. "From the Irish Arts Centre," she said faintly. "In New York."

Maeve moved closer to the lamp and peered at the brochure. Lots of lovely photos and promotional blather, then one section in boldface print.

Call for Artists
For the Upcoming Exhibit, "Into the West"
Fine Arts from the West of Ireland

HER PULSE POUNDING, she handed the brochure back to Declan. "Would you look at this."

He scanned the text, a slow smile blooming on his tired face. "I think you're meant to send this crowd some of your paintings, Mam. If you want to start a new life, here's your chance."

Maeve couldn't speak. Hazel…what miracles the girl had wrought. Then Declan turned the brochure over. "Wait—Hazel's written a bit of a note here." He showed her a scribble in the margin. *Declan, your present is arriving later—you'll know it when you see it.* "Any notion what she means?"

Whatever it is, thought Maeve, *it'll be exactly what you need.* "I haven't a clue," she finally said. "Still, we've made out pretty well tonight, haven't we? Three lovely gifts."

"You'd think we've had the Three Wise Men visit us, to help us find Christmas," said Declan.

"Not Three Wise Men," said Maeve, her heart full. "Just one very wise girl."

SPECIAL BONUS EXCERPT OF BECOMING EMMA

If you'd like to know more about what happened to Hazel that Christmas, here's a brief sample of my 6th Irish novel *Becoming Emma*, featuring Hazel's elder sister Emma

This full-length novel begins the year before *The Christmas Visitor*...

CHAPTER 1

Becoming Emma

This couldn't be right.

Emma Carey paused on the footpath and stared up at the stately Victorian house, the gray and amber exterior glowing in the morning light. Surely this historic mansion, adorned with turrets and gingerbread and a weathervane shaped like a whimsical half-moon, couldn't be her new workplace!

Only moments before, striding from a bus stop in downtown Mount Belleford, Washington, Emma had been filled with anticipation. On this sunny August day, the breeze off nearby Belleford Bay was soft and cool against her flushed face. Crossing the street, she caught a glimpse of the snow-capped peak of Boulder Mountain, looming to the east above the dark green foothills surrounding the town.

Yet now that she was supposedly at her destination—a nonprofit Irish cultural center—all the beauty of her new city didn't ease her tension. Peering at her mobile, Emma realized she was running late despite the assiduous use of a new scheduling app.

Plus she kept looking around for office buildings, but saw nothing but impeccably maintained older homes with manicured lawns.

She checked the directions again on her mobile: the Ireland Place office was at 13 Parkland Circle. And an elegant little sign on the lawn confirmed it:

13 Parkland Circle

What was she meant to do now?

Emma's heart pounded with nerves. If only she'd done a reconnaissance mission yesterday! Her younger sister Hazel had suggested it—well, not really *suggested*, since the girl wasn't a great one for giving advice. But she did email Emma with an extremely mild remark, that it mightn't hurt to nip over to her new workplace before her first day, to get the lay of the land. And as a veteran of many new jobs in faraway locales, Hazel was one to know these things.

All the same, by now Emma was running so behind schedule that she'd no choice but to ask for directions.

With her new, decisive personality (she'd acquired it only weeks ago, after her thirty-first birthday, so she wasn't quite up to speed with being forceful and assertive) she hurried up the footpath. At home in Dublin, knocking on a stranger's door was no big deal: someone would actually open it, *smile* at you, give you the direction you needed, *and* ask you in for a cup of tea.

Passing a mass of cream hydrangeas in full bloom, Emma clutched her handbag, climbing the entryway stairs to the porch as fast as her pencil skirt and new ankle boots would allow. Straightening her blazer, she pinned on what she hoped was a friendly yet professional expression, and made herself reach for the doorbell. *Oh, God, I'll make a crap first impression, and it'll be no one's fault but my own...*

Before she could press the bell, the door swung open. "You

must be Emma?" said an attractive, fortyish brunette, her lustrous hair almost hiding her wireless headset. "The new girl?"

"So I *have* come to the right place," said Emma, hoping her own carefully-styled hairdo wasn't standing on end, after her rushing about. "I'm terribly sorry I'm late, the scheduling app I tried out was banjaxed, and the house didn't look at all like a business—"

"Ah, no worries," said the woman with a Irish accent. She smilingly ushered Emma inside. "It always throws folk new to Ireland Place. Besides, we're on Irish time here."

"Good to know," said Emma. "So tardiness is not only tolerated, but sometimes... encouraged?"

"That's it. By the way, I'm Lakshmi. From County Monaghan."

"Emma Carey. Dublin." She gazed at the house's foyer, rendered nearly speechless with awe. Golden wood wainscoting lent warmth to the otherwise dim space, and an imposing staircase with a hefty, curved bannister soared upward. Displayed above a vintage, roll-top desk was a large Irish flag, and on the desk sat a name plate, placed front and center: *Lakshmi O'Toole, Office Manager.*

"The house is quite a pile, isn't it?" said Lakshmi ruefully. "Built by some timber magnate back in the 1890s."

"It's quite stunning," said Emma, trying to act blasé, instead of gobsmacked.

"Patrick—from County Kildare, by the way—was determined to give our little island of Irishness some amazing digs. But I tell you, the rent will make your eyes water."

Lakshmi led Emma past her desk. "Patrick's office," she said in the doorway of what must have originally served as the front room. "Since our esteemed director is guiding *the* hub of Irish arts and culture on the West coast," she added, an ironic glint in her eye, "naturally he needs a 'lord of the Irish manor' vibe."

Lined with bookshelves, Patrick Delahanty's lair had floor to ceiling, lace-curtained windows, an old-fashioned, chintz-covered divan against the far wall, and a massive, leather-tooled desk twice the size of Lakshmi's taking up the entire middle of the room. "He's…er, in a meeting at the moment, downtown."

"That's all right," said Emma, relieved that she wouldn't encounter the boss just yet. She'd met Patrick only twice, in Seattle, but found him a bit overpowering. "Gives me time to settle in."

"You saw my reception desk in the foyer," said Lakshmi, "but it's only for show—I do most of my work in there." Pointing into a small anteroom, containing modern office furniture and a desktop computer, she said wryly, "Patrick was set to get all the staff antique desks too, but Mr. Clancy, our accountant, put his foot down."

"I imagine the cost made *his* eyes water," said Emma, smiling. She liked her new colleague already.

"Oh, *nothing* makes Mr. Clancy cry," said Lakshmi in a confiding tone, leading Emma across the foyer. "Though our new kitchen appliances came close. Let me show you—wait, I've a call." A pause. "Speak of the devil! I'd better take it." She stepped into her anteroom.

While she waited, Emma smoothed her hair, glad she'd just had her streaky tawny-brown color touched up. Then she pulled out her mobile and rather vengefully deleted the app that had made her late—one of many she hadn't been able to figure out. Maybe it was okay that she wasn't an app sort of person. And that oftentimes, she simply didn't *get* a lot of technology.

She peeked in at Lakshmi, whose eyes were glued to a large mobile phone on a stand while she pounded on her keyboard. Emma had to wonder: did her brain not work like other people's, those super organized sorts who felt entirely easy relying on their mobiles and other tech for *everything*, including mental and emotional sustenance?

Or did she have a bigger problem? Maybe she'd inherited

her short attention span from her mam, who flitted—maybe more like lurched—from one project to the next without completing any of them.

Or maybe, thought Emma, she was, at heart, an old-fashioned girl like her younger sister Hazel?

Emma jammed her mobile (minus the narky app) back into her handbag. Time management hadn't mattered at her previous, short-lived job: co-running The Little Irish Gift Shop in Seattle. Working all hours, she had no time *to* manage.

But being a first-time *executive*...Emma gazed admiringly around the mansion's foyer again. She vowed then and there she would learn from her experience back at the gift shop: the topsy-turvy schedule, the leadership vacuum, and her lack of... she pondered how to put this...*personal discipline*, that was it. Likewise, the office politics that had done her no favors.

Not that the shop had had a proper office to have politics *in*, and she'd had absolutely no choice but to leave that job anyway.

But still.

And here at Ireland Place, if she was on the leadership team, at least she'd be sure to have her own desk...

Moments later, Lakshmi emerged. "Sorry about that—you do *not* let Himself go to voice mail. Where were we?"

"The kitchen?" said Emma. If "Himself" was Mr. Clancy, she guessed *he* called the shots here, not Patrick. "With the appliances that almost made an accountant cry?"

"This way," said Lakshmi, leading her into a bright kitchen. "Patrick had to have green, of course."

At the sight of the mint green, retro-style fridge, microwave and cooker, Emma's eyes widened. "Oh, so cute!"

"The dining room's through there," said her companion, waving beyond the kitchen. "Comes in handy for meetings." Emma caught a glimpse of a long, antique dining table polished to a high sheen, before Lakshmi swept her up the grand staircase to a roomy, high-ceilinged landing.

She paused at a massive wardrobe against one wall. "Office supplies, help yourself," said Lakshmi, then quickly introduced Emma to slew of co-workers: a rumpled IT trio occupying a large room full of laptop-strewn tables, and another adjoining room of interns.

They didn't look much older than Hazel, maybe their early twenties, and they all had Irish voices—Patrick apparently *did* only hire people from home. As they smiled, saying "Grand meeting you, Emma," and one even threw in a *"Failté,"* Emma felt ten times more welcome than she had at any other job.

"Even if you lot are on your best behavior at the moment," said Lakshmi, looking at them sternly, "consider yourselves warned. You'll show Emma some proper respect, even if she's not that much older than you are."

"Yes, Missus," chorused the interns.

"How many times do I have to tell you, don't call me that!" snapped Lakshmi, though Emma was sure she was hiding a smile. "One more time and heads will *roll*."

"Right, *Mam*," said an IT guy. Lakshmi narrowed her eyes at him, then took Emma across the hall to a closed door, murmuring, "God, the *cheek*. You've no idea how good it is to have another grownup round here."

Emma wondered if that meant Patrick *wasn't* a grownup. Then she forgot all about it, stopping in her tracks as she saw the name plate on the door:

Emma Carey
Special Projects Coordinator

Simply *seeing* her title gave her a thrill, and as Lakshmi opened the door with a flourish, Emma gazed appreciatively at her new domain. She'd have not only her own desk, but her own office! In addition to the adjustable desk and ergonomic chair, there was a brand-new laptop along with a second, oversized screen. As she glanced at the window, her eyes widened. "And a view too!"

"You like it?" said Lakshmi. "It might compensate a bit for your skinny pay packet."

Emma laughed. Sure, her Ireland Place salary would be modest, but it was way better than her previous pay at the gift shop. She pulled aside the lace curtain to admire the sight of the bay, waves sparkling, and the gray-green islands beyond. "It's gorgeous."

Stepping to her desk, Emma resisted the urge to caress the smooth, silvery laptop (she'd wait until she was alone), and noticed the stack of composition notebooks, expensive ones, like you'd get at a stationer's shop. She couldn't help asking, "These are for *me?*"

"Patrick guessed you were a paper sort of person," said Lakshmi, "and believes jotting down your every thought will facilitate creativity and problem-solving."

"Oh," said Emma, pleased. She wouldn't have thought Patrick to be that perceptive. "He must've noticed all my sticky notes at the gift shop."

"He'll want you to jot down *his* every thought too. Anyway, there's lots more notebooks in the wardrobe, and we've a lifetime supply of sticky notes too," said Lakshmi. "Feel free to bring whatever you need home."

"Really?" Emma cast a covetous look at the stack. She did have a thing for notebooks.

"The laptop too. You might as well know, Patrick is a great one for getting people to take work home." Lakshmi rolled her eyes. "That doesn't mean you have to go for it."

Emma didn't want to admit that being new to Mount Belleford, she hadn't a whole lot on. She *certainly* had no plans to see her old mate Fitz or her frenemy, Maire, from the gift shop. She said carefully, "Oh, I won't mind working evenings now and then."

"Right, I'll leave you to it," said Lakshmi. "Patrick should be back soon—he wants to show you the top floor himself." She suddenly frowned. "Do you smell doughnuts?" She strode across the hall. "Gerry, Martin, it's a bit early for elevenses, you Hobbits!"

"We were hungry," Emma heard one of the boys say.

"You're always hungry," said Lakshmi. "I just wish you'd eat downstairs—and put that lovely dining table Patrick bought you to some use."

"But then we'd never get any work done," someone else said.

"Well, I don't see you getting anything done *now*," she retorted. Returning to the doorway, Lakshmi gave Emma an exasperated glance that seemed to say, *You see what I put up with?* Then she headed down the stairs.

Emma recalled being late today, and got mortified all over again. People on executive tracks were *never* late! Really, she'd nearly mucked up the most important day of her career—that is, she *would* have mucked it up if Ireland Place wasn't such a relaxed sort of organization.

She picked up a notebook—she would create a proper schedule for herself straightaway—then turned on the laptop. Adjusting her super-comfy chair, Emma smiled at her screen. She was going to *love* working here. In fact, she was entirely sure she'd never be homesick for Ireland again. And with such an auspicious start to her new job, she just *knew* her second go at rebooting her life in America would be an unparalleled success.

In that moment, Emma doubled-down on the first of the three vows she'd made before leaving the gift shop: *I will **kill** at this new job.* As for the other two (and far less important ones, concerning romantic entanglements), well, those vows didn't apply. Absolutely not.

She would make *certain* of that...

You'll find more about Emma and the O'Donoghue family in Susan's latest book of the Ballydara series, ***The Fairy Cottage of Ballydara**...Becoming Emma* and and all the Ballydara novels are available in ebook online or by request at your local library!

ABOUT THE AUTHOR

Susan Colleen Browne is a graduate of the College of the Environment, Western Washington University. She's the author of an award-winning memoir, *Little Farm in the Foothills,* and other Little Farm books, including her popular food gardening guide, *Little Farm in the Garden.*

Susan weaves her love of Ireland and her passion for country living into her Village of Ballydara series, novels and stories of love, friendship and family set in the Irish countryside. Her latest Irish novel is **The Fairy Cottage of Ballydara**, with more books on the way!

She has also created a fantasy-adventure series for tweens set near Seattle. A community college instructor, Susan runs a little homestead with her husband John in the Foothills of the Pacific Northwest, USA.

When Susan isn't wrangling chickens or tending vegetable beds, she's working on her next book… You can connect with Susan at her newsletter, **This Little Farm Life**!

BOOKS BY SUSAN COLLEEN BROWNE

The Village of Ballydara Series

It Only Takes Once, Book 1 (print and ebook)

Mother Love, Book 2 (print and ebook)

The Hopeful Romantic, Book 3 (print and ebook)

The Galway Girls, Book 4 (print and ebook)

The Secret Well, short story ebook

A Christmas Visitor, short story ebook

The Little Irish Gift Shop, Book 5 (print and ebook)

Becoming Emma, Book 6 (print and ebook)

Becoming Emma, Special Edition (ebook)

The Fairy Cottage of Ballydara, Book 7 (ebook)

Little Farm in the Foothills Series

Little Farm in the Foothills: A Boomer Couple's Search for the Slow Life, Book 1 (print and ebook)

Little Farm Homegrown: A Memoir of Food-Growing, Midlife, and Self-Reliance on a Small Homestead, Book 2 (print and ebook)

Little Farm in the Garden: A Practical Mini-Guide to Raising Selected Fruits and Vegetables Homestead-Style, Book 3 (print and ebook)

Little Farm in the Henhouse: A True-Life Tale of Hen-Keeping, Homestead-Style, Book 4 (print and ebook)

Little Farm for the Holidays: Celebrating the Christmas Season, Homestead-Style, Book 5 (print and ebook)

The Morgan Carey Series for Tweens, set in the Pacific Northwest

Morgan Carey and The Curse of the Corpse Bride, Book 1, a lighthearted Halloween story (print and ebook)

Morgan Carey and The Mystery of the Christmas Fairies, Book 2, a gentle fantasy (print and ebook), set in the Foothills!

The Secret Astoria Scavenger Hunt, Book 3, a haunted house adventure (print and ebook)

All the books are available for **free** in ebook and print format at your local library by request, or you can use an ebook library app. You can also order them from your neighborhood bookstore or find them at your favorite online retailer.

Thank you for letting my stories, true and imaginary, be part of your Christmas!

All my best for the holidays and always,

Susan

www.ingramcontent.com/pod-product-compliance
Lightning Source LLC
Chambersburg PA
CBHW032138040426
42449CB00005B/295